MW00698380

I Accuse

Jimmy Carter and
the Rise of
Militant Islam

Philip Pilevsky

Printed in the United States of America.

For information address:

Durban House Publishing Company, Inc.
7502 Greenville Avenue, Suite 500, Dallas, Texas 75231

Library of Congress Cataloging-in-Publication Data

Pilevsky, Philip, 1946 –

I Accuse: Jimmy Carter and the Rise of Militant Islam /
Philip Pilevsky

Library of Congress Control Number: 2003105046

p. cm.

ISBN 1-930754-38-8

First Edition

10 9 8 7 6 5 4 3 2 1

Visit our Web site at
http://www.durbanhouse.com

To my father, to whom I owe everything.

Acknowledgements

I want to thank Kenneth Shouler of Wordsworth Writing and Editing in Harrison, New York, for his research, persistence, and overall editing help with this manuscript.

Contents

Introduction

In 1989 the Soviet Union was completing its retreat from Afghanistan, which it had invaded a decade earlier. Most Americans applauded Afghanistan's "victory," having hoped for the Soviets to fail in their attempted conquest of their Muslim neighbor. I realized that in adopting the Afghan cause, Americans were on the wrong side of history, a point made clearer as the war ended. Radical Islam had gained its first base of operations following the 1979 revolution in Iran; now it owned another. For the second time in ten years the United States had assisted militant Islam in securing a foothold in the world.

In 1988 I wrote the following letter to the *Wall Street Journal*:

The Soviet Union appears ready to have its troops retreat from Afghanistan, leaving a puppet Communist-influenced government in Kabul fending for itself. This political charade has led the United States to believe that "we won the war."

Ironically, the United States has potentially put the worst kind of fascist ideology in power. The United States has, with a multibillion-dollar budget, encouraged the Soviets to relinquish significant control and instead left Afghanistan open to the potential of becoming a second militant Islamic fundamentalist state.

Without Soviet backing or U.S. defense, the Najibullah government will surely fall, paving the way for the fundamentalist *mujahidin* to seize control.

Therefore, indirectly, the United States has left Afghanistan wide open to accept a government which, if it resembles Iran, should become the antithesis of all the U.S. should and would be fighting to uphold: democracy, free will, human rights. The United States has not only lost the war, but has also given Islamic fundamentalism a helping hand.

The recent rise of Islamic fundamentalism, from an insignificant fringe phenomenon to a major state influencing world politics, has been, to say the least, alarming. The state of Iran under Khomeini has given Islamic fundamentalism a legitimacy and a voice in world affairs. The problems in dealing with Iran have unhinged the United States domestically and internationally over the past decade. For the United States to have laid the foundations for a second Islamic fundamentalist state, inadvertently, one assumes, is a heinous crime, not only against democracy, but against the stability of world politics in general.

Afghanistan in the 1980s became to the Islamic world what the Spanish Civil War was to the Communists: it created an international brotherhood of fighting men, a new version of the Lincoln Brigade, well versed in the ways of terrorism. This movement venerates a despotic government: lacking reason to guide man and human potential, rather man's destiny is in the hands of God. Civilized political thought is replaced by irrational religious fervor. There is no vocabulary for analysis and speculation, but rather an unrealistic language of poetry in this militant revolutionary movement. Militant Islamic fundamentalism stifles the mind, which leads to blind passivity and lack of initiative; man is relieved of all responsibility. In short, militant Islamic fundamentalism is difficult to comprehend, elusive to deal with, and formidable in its strength.

The United States can have dialogue with the Soviets; however, all communications between militant Islamic fundamentalists and a Western power are improbable, and negotiations are and will continue to be futile. Ironically, the Soviets, in the light of dealing with militant Islamic fundamentalists, now appear sane and predictable. The U.S. and the West can be sure of not only being portrayed as Satan, but of having to deal with ruthless, unpredictable, and wildly fanatic theocracies should Islamic fundamentalism gain control.

Indeed, Islamic fundamentalism as a transnational unifying power is replacing nationalism as the moving force behind change in the late 20th century. Nationalistic sentiment in both Russia and China was able to turn Marxism on its head, but the word of Allah reverberates throughout Lebanon, Syria, Saudi Arabia, Egypt, Iraq, and Pakistan, as well as other governments with large Muslim populations. Secularist rulers of these countries need only look toward the deposed Shah and the hung liberals of Iran and the now-retreating Soviet army to know what might await them in their own lands. Citizens of Muslim countries, including Afghanistan, need only look at the reign of terror in Iran to recognize their own fate. Sadly, the well-meaning democratic United States set out eight years ago to truncate Soviet expansion and succeeded in igniting another time bomb.

The response of the editor to my assistant was dismissive: "We won't be able to use Mr. Pilevsky's article on Afghanistan, but we'd be happy to consider other opinion pieces, particularly in the areas of real estate or mall development [real estate being my occupation]. Thank you for thinking of the *Journal*."

The letter I sent might have been commonplace ten, or even fifteen, years later. But in 1988, I believe the argument I advanced was prescient. At the time I voiced my views frequently as a regular guest on New York television stations, including FOX and WPIX. I also lectured at NYU and sounded out members of the Foreign Policy Association. It was apparent to me that the popular beat-the-Soviets-and-you-have-won thinking embraced by the West was already old thinking. It also seemed apparent that Afghanistan would become a separate but parallel universe for the runaway growth of Islamism. Not only was it a second Islamic state, but I knew that the witches' brew of terrorists —comprising a veritable camp for terrorists in Afghanistan—would give the United States and its allies a different, and in many ways greater, challenge than they'd ever experienced.

Afghanistan was an effect of what some medievalists call an intermediate cause. It was that cause—of the growing

Islamist political movement in Afghanistan—that interested me most.

In the late 1970s, in the years before Iran's Islamic revolution, Islamic fundamentalism was a fringe phenomenon, a generally innocuous force in the world—a veritable brushfire of a nuisance that would flare up, only to be doused when repressive Arab regimes showed the determination to avenge its occasionally violent deeds. Islamic radicalism was a tactical movement, lacking the overarching philosophical and religious weight of the worldwide militant Islamism to come.

Then came a change in the U.S. policy toward Iran's leader, the shah, Mohammed Reza Pahlavi. The United States demanded radical changes in the way Iran's internal affairs were conducted. In early 1977, at the dawn of President Carter's administration, Secretary of State Cyrus Vance reminded the shah that human rights played an important role in Carter's policy. The administration asked the shah to institute the right of free assembly, even as the monarchy was fighting a war on another front: the Soviet Union was stepping up a campaign of propaganda, espionage, and even sabotage inside Iran, and Islamic fundamentalists were collaborating with Iran's communist Tudeh Party to overthrow the government. The Carter administration linked arms sales to human rights concessions, reducing sales of AWACs (airborne warning system) aircraft to Iran. [1] In another instance, Pat Derian, the chief proponent of the cause of human rights in the Department of State, refused to help the shah acquire the tear gas that he needed. She and some of her assistants were utterly unsympathetic to his need for assistance, and thus were aligned with his opponents. [2]

The shah didn't think it was appropriate for the United States to concern itself with Iran's domestic situation. The shah thought that the solution to problems such as the increasing chaos of Iranian society "depended on his personal decision." [3]

The shah had enjoyed closer relationships with Republicans in the White House. This was especially true of Richard Nixon. The shah surmised that Republicans were better able to understand the delicate balance needed to rule Iran. The monarchy had to do its part to lead the country out of its underdevelopment, but needed to maintain authoritarian rule in order to accomplish that aim. Thus America's chief diplomat in the Nixon administration, Secretary of State Henry Kissinger, appreciated the progress that the shah had made in a short period of time.

In contrast, Carter preached the sermon of human rights. Indeed, Carter made human rights the centerpiece of foreign policy. "In large measure, the beginnings of the modern concept of human rights go back to the laws and the Prophets of the Judeo-Christian traditions," he told the World Jewish Congress on November 2, 1977. "I've been steeped in the Bible since early childhood, and I believe that anyone who reads the ancient words of the Old Testament will find … the idea of equality before the law and the supremacy of law over the whims of any ruler; the idea of the dignity of the individual human being and also the individual conscience; the ideas of service to the poor and to the oppressed; the ideas of self-government and tolerance and of nations living together in peace, despite differences of belief." [4]

Carter traced his own sensitivity to human rights to his upbringing in South Georgia. "As a child, I rode a bus to school each day with the other white students, while the black students walked, and never gave a thought to the lack of equality inherent in the separateness," he writes in his autobiography. [5]

So it was only natural that, four months after his inauguration, he gave a pointed address on foreign affairs at the University of Notre Dame. "It is a new world that calls for a new American foreign policy—a policy based on constant decency in its values and on optimism in our historical vision," he said at the commencement. [6]

The expectation was noble, but in its own way absurd: how could this Persian monarchy measure up to the representative governments of the West, such as the United States and Great Britain?

Still, Carter believed that he had a mandate to effect change. He had won the presidency in 1976 for several reasons. Disenchantment with the Republican Party could be traced to Nixon's 1974 resignation and the subsequent pardon by Gerald Ford. The loss of nearly 60,000 soldiers in Vietnam had turned the populace against any further foreign intervention. As a political outsider, Carter had promised to reform politics as usual in Washington and lend some clarity to a time of confusion in foreign policy. He would have an "open" administration, unlike the secretive Nixon regime, which ended in flames.

It became clear early in his presidency that Carter's foreign policy was an extension of his own moralistic views. Like Woodrow Wilson 65 years earlier, Carter believed that all people owned the right to self-determination. Carter's moralism has been described as "all-pervasive."

He wrote in his *Memoirs*,

I was familiar with the widely accepted arguments that we had to choose between idealism and
realism, or between morality and the exertion of
power; but I rejected those claims. To me, the
demonstration of American idealism was a practical
and realistic approach to foreign affairs, and moral
principles were the best foundation for the exertion
of American power and influence. [7]

Carter held firmly to the belief that man possessed
the ability "through God's mediation to become a better
person."[8] However, with his personal moral and religious
beliefs and principles guiding his actions, he seemed to
lack the aura of leadership that Americans desire to see in
their commander-in-chief.

This uneasy fit in Washington didn't stop Carter from
applying his ideas to foreign policy. At the same commencement address at the University of Notre Dame he said,

I believe we can have a foreign policy that is
democratic, that is based on fundamental values, and
that uses power and influence, which we have, for
humane purposes. We can also have a foreign policy
that the American people support and, for a change,
know and understand. . . . Because we know that
democracy works we can reject the arguments of
those rulers who deny human rights to their people. [9]

In the view of the Carter administration, the last sentiment applied to the shah of Iran. Vance shared Carter's
policy of compassion. He, too, was concerned with a world
full of suffering and believed that U.S. foreign policy could

ameliorate it. To Carter and Vance, the shah's ironclad grip on power was incompatible with the human rights of his citizenry. Their view, however, was not fully supported by the facts.

While the shah often scoffed at Islamic clerics, deriding them as "lice-ridden mullahs" or, in a reference to their dark clothing, "black reactionaries," the Carter administration considered the clerics sympathetic figures yearning for freedom, democracy, and basic human rights.

The Carter administration viewed mullahs as an impetus to freedom. Indeed, some administration figures managed to attribute lofty motives to Ayatollah Khomeini. The U.S. ambassador to Iran, William Sullivan, once referred to Khomeini as a "Gandhi-like" figure. [10] Carter's representative to the United Nations, Andrew Young, held the aged cleric in similar esteem, deeming him "some kind of saint."

Such views not only grossly misrepresented Khomeini, as time and events would confirm, but failed to appreciate the progress in Iran under the shah, whose initiatives included increased rights for women, land reform favoring peasants, and expanded educational opportunities.

For a time it seemed that the shah's efforts at liberalizing Iran satisfied Washington. On a trip to Iran at the end of 1977, the American president proclaimed in a toast, "Iran, because of the great leadership of the shah, is an island of stability in one of the more troubled regions of the world." He added, "The cause of human rights is one that also is shared deeply by our people and by the leaders of our two nations." [11] The shah, meanwhile, told *Business Week*, "Carter looks like a smart man. . . . I think we can cooperate with the Carter Administration." [12] Stunned and embittered by Carter's performance, Iran's moderate opposition groups, which had long regarded the shah as "America's puppet," turned more sharply than ever away from the United States. [13]

But bold words from Carter were not matched by bold actions. The shah had been a staunch ally of the United States for some 35 years, during which he had enjoyed the support of seven successive presidents. Eventually, however, through its failure to support this longtime friend when deeds counted more than words, the Carter administration would contribute to the Iranian revolution and the fateful creation of the Islamic Republic of Iran. The consequences of Carter's inaction are still felt years later.

I argue here that the colossal failure of the Carter administration with respect to Iran occurred in four distinct but overlapping stages. The first of these lasted from Carter's inauguration, in January 1977, following his defeat of Gerald Ford in the election, to the beginning of 1978. During this year the administration failed to heed the winds of change blowing across Iran. These changes were manifest in protests, invariably clerically driven, and generally more strident attacks on the monarchy than had previously occurred during the shah's reign. Despite the determined opposition faced by the monarchy and the shah's eagerness for American approval and support, Vance worried that "Many in the Carter administration, particularly President Carter, considered [the shah] a tyrant." [14] Preoccupied with the shah's adherence to its human rights policy, the Carter White House shrank from providing the firm support that the shah had received from Nixon and Kissinger, who viewed the Iranian monarch as a vital surrogate for American power in the Persian Gulf.[15]

In the second stage, the changes in Iran were far easier to detect and, therefore, to respond to. In January 1978, police fired on religious demonstrators in the city of Qum who were angered by a newspaper article defaming Khomeini that appeared in the government-controlled press. The article, apparently approved by the shah, was entitled "Black and Red Imperialism" (referring to the black garments of the mullahs, or religious leaders, and the communists). A mix of facts and opinions, the article attacked Khomeini personally. As soon as the paper reached Qom, people rushed to the streets to demonstrate, shouting "Long Live Khomeini" and "Death to [Mohammed Reza] Pahlavi's [shah of Iran] Rule." Several people were killed, including members of the clergy who quickly attained the status of "martyr." The Shiite custom of honoring martyrs for 40 days after their death resulted in sustained and violent demonstrations.

Vance, noting that the demonstrations were increasingly xenophobic, anti-Western, anti-American, and anti-Semitic, reported to Carter on May 10 that the incidents amounted to "the most serious anti-shah activities in Iran since 1963," when Khomeini had led an opposition movement's attempt to overthrow the monarchy.[16] A year later the shah had Khomeini exiled to Turkey, from which the ayatollah subsequently moved to Iraq. Despite Vance's report, however, no action was taken to quell the unrest. Carter's words just weeks before, about Iran being an "island in a sea of stability," were badly misinformed and now certainly outdated.

The protests continued through the fall of 1978, sometimes drawing crowds of several hundred thousand. The shah's regime was clearly threatened, yet Washington refused to intervene on behalf of its most loyal ally in the region.

Why? Vance depicts an administration preoccupied with other matters. "It would not be correct to assume . . . that prior to September [1978] the situation in Iran was a subject of daily concern to the president or me," he wrote.[17] He recalls a White House that in August 1978 was preoccupied with the Camp David summit on the Middle East; Vance himself devoted much of October and November to the summit's Egyptian-Israeli negotiations. Given his May 10 report to Carter, it is difficult to reconcile his initial concern with his later distraction. At the very least, the administration misjudged the urgency of the shah's plight.

It is arguable that bringing together Egyptian president Anwar el-Sadat and Israeli Prime Minister Menachem Begin in September of 1978 was Carter's foreign policy apex. These delicate Camp David meetings, extending over 13 days, were conducted in the attempt to gain a lasting peace.

The main issue was the Israeli settlements in Sinai and Old Jerusalem established after the Six-Day War in 1967. Now Sadat wanted a commitment that Israeli forces would withdraw from Egyptian territory. But on the tenth day, when shown a draft of an agreement, Sadat could not accept it. Carter recalls that Sadat saw the settlements as a "precondition" of any agreement and that "He would negotiate on *when* they would be withdrawn, not *if* they could be withdrawn." They had reached an impasse.

"I could not think of any way to resolve this fundamental difference between the Israelis and the Egyptians," Carter remembered. "On the Sinai settlements, Begin did not stand alone among his delegation. So far as I could tell, the Israelis were united in their belief that the settlers must not be moved." [18]

Carter faced the grim prospects:

> That evening I began to list the differences be-
> tween the two nations, and was heartbroken to see
> how relatively insignificant they really were, com-
> pared to the great advantages of peace. I sat on the
> back terrace late into the night, but could think of
> no way to make further progress. My only decision
> was that all of us should work together to leave
> Camp David in as positive a mood as possible, tak-
> ing credit for what we had done and resolved to con-
> tinue our common search for an elusive accord. [19]

Thus on Friday, September 15, 1978, Carter recalls,

> I awoke to the realization that we could go no
> further. I called the American delegation in Aspen,
> and we discussed how to deal with our failure. ...I
> instructed staff members to begin drafting an out-
> line of a speech for me to make to Congress, ex-
> plaining what we had attempted at Camp David
> during the two weeks and why we had not been suc-
> cessful. [20]

After being informed by Cyrus Vance that Sadat was requesting a helicopter to leave, Carter confronted Sadat about the consequences of failure for Egypt and the United States. The confrontation led to movement on the key issues. On the thirteenth day a treaty was signed. Israel agreed to return the Sinai to Egypt, a transfer that would be completed in 1982. In a joint letter the two nations also agreed to negotiate Palestinian autonomy measures in the Israeli-occupied West Bank and Gaza Strip, but virtually no progress was made on this issue until the 1990s. In 1978, Sadat would share the Nobel Peace Prize with Menachem Begin.

But the agreement did not bring about peace with the other Arab countries. Instead it led increasingly to Egypt's being isolated from its Arab neighbors. Three years later, in October 1981, Sadat was assassinated by Muslim extremists, who were opposed to the peace initiative with Israel.

On November 3, 1978, the shah called the White House to request the president's opinion about whether he should form a military or a coalition government to counter the unrest. In response, the administration dispatched Ambassador Sullivan to assure the shah that it supported him "without reservation." In actuality, this was but a nominal commitment, as it included no specific advice about what action the shah should take. To Carter's national security adviser, Zbigniew Brzezinski, this lack of specificity meant that the State Department (Brzezinski's frequent adversary in the matter of Iran policy) had given up on the shah and was "soft" on any sort of military response to the turmoil in Iran. [21]

From Vance's admission that "We would not attempt to tell the shah how to deal with his own internal political problems," two conclusions might be reached. First, the Carter administration had freely urged the shah to liberalize Iranian society, although this stance contradicted Vance's stated position on interference in Iran's internal problems. Second, the administration knew that the shah had been diagnosed with lymphoma. Since the shah was demonstrably averse to taking decisive action even before his illness, it would have been logical to assume that now, in illness, he was in even greater need of direct guidance and assistance in handling his domestic problems.

By November 9 Sullivan had sent a message to Washington warning that the administration must begin "thinking the unthinkable." In essence, he asked what the United States would do if the shah and the military proved unable to govern. While the message agreed with the State Department analysis of the situation, there was in the White House, in Vance's words, "a brooding fear that any action that implied we did not expect the shah to survive would contribute to the paralysis of will and stimulate the opposition to increased violence."[22]

But the shah's paralysis of will was matched by that of the Carter administration. After all, doing nothing to support the shah—other than issuing noncommittal statements of "support without reservation"—would surely hasten his end. If the shah, who had enacted martial law in order to remain in power, lacked sufficient will, so too did the Carter administration, which had analyzed the alarming situation in Iran and still taken no decisive action.

Some observers came to see Carter's ambivalence as a trait of his character. Pierre Salinger wrote:

In matters of foreign policy, Jimmy Carter was really two persons. There was a public and a private Jimmy Carter. The result of any foreign policy negotiation depended on which Jimmy Carter you were dealing with. Almost to a man, the heads of state who had dealings with Carter came to admire him.

They considered him highly intelligent, and found him better prepared than almost anyone else at the negotiating table. And yet, some of the public pronouncements Carter would make five or six days after the meetings were seen by these same leaders as erratic in the light of the agreements they had reached, and would all but annul the high regard the leaders had developed for Carter in private. [23]

Despite this kind of waffling, there is no denying that Carter achieved certain foreign policy objectives. The Panama Canal treaty created good will with a hemispheric neighbor, and the accord between Egypt and Israel advanced the cause of peace in the Middle East. In both instances Carter remained fixed on a central idea and focused on a central objective. In other cases, however, in which he failed to pursue this strategy, the results were abysmal.

One such instance was his attempt to convince Western European nations to approve U.S. development of the neutron bomb in order to offset the Soviet Union's overwhelming advantage in conventional forces. Carter thus persuaded German chancellor Helmut Schmidt, who had been reluctant to support the bomb's development because of his Socialist Party's opposition to military buildups. Schmidt finally endorsed the policy, only to have Carter decide not to build the neutron bomb after all. Carter's inexplicable about-face effectively ended the relationship between himself and Schmidt, who came to despise him. In the case of Iran, Carter's inconsistency was surely a problem.

During his campaign for the presidency, Jimmy Carter rebuked the Nixon and Ford administrations for their record of enormous arms sales throughout the world. Said

Carter, "I am particularly concerned by our nation's role as the world's leading arms salesman. How can we be both the world's leading champion of peace and the world's leading supplier of the weapons of war?" Four months after his inauguration he announced a new restrained arms transfer policy and a tough set of sales restrictions relevant to all countries except those with which the United States had major defense agreements. The exceptions included the NATO countries, Japan, Australia, New Zealand, and Israel. Iran was omitted.

Not two months later, on July 7, Carter presented Congress with a proposal to sell Iran seven highly sophisticated flying radar systems consisting of Boeing 707 jet airplanes equipped with 30-foot diameter mushroom-like radar scanners sprouting from their bodies. It was at the time the most expensive aircraft system the United States had ever developed. The proposed AWACS package was nothing less than an astonishing presidential about-face and shocked Carter's liberal allies in Congress. It also contributed to Carter's growing image of inconsistency and unpredictability.

Jimmy Carter had already expressed his disapproval of "Lone Ranger" tactics with respect to Iran. While Vance claims that he "did not rule out support for a military government that would restore order and put an end to bloodshed," he maintained that the United States should not make such a decision for Iran. In fact, Vance agreed with Carter that the shah should avoid the use of an "iron fist" to restore order, and further believed that an army that was 50 percent conscripted could not be relied upon to accomplish that goal. Finally, both the president and his secretary of state opposed a military crackdown as being antithetical to what the Carter administration stood for.

According to *Foreign Affairs*, the Carter administration was often distinguished from its predecessors "by dint of its rhetoric, its manner and style, and of course its moralism. But these differences, though significant, do no go to the substance of policy." In the view of analyst Robert W. Tucker, the litmus test was based on what the Carter administration was willing "to risk in blood and treasure to achieve its foreign policy objectives. The brief answer is that it was willing to risk considerably less than its predecessors had been willing to risk."[24]

The third stage of the administration's failure in Iran involved other missed opportunities for action. By early 1979 the imminent exile of the shah and the return from exile of Ayatollah Khomeini after 14 years presented yet another opening for Carter to implement a strategy to either save the monarchy, support a new, more moderate government, or initiate contact with the shah's opponents. Carter did none of these, failing to heed either the advice of his State Department, National Security Council, or ambassador to Iran or dire predictions by Israel and France of the shah's impending fall. Without a strategy in place, the United States was an outsider, utterly without influence, as a revolution swept Iran and a xenophobic theocracy, profoundly hostile to American interests, seized power.

The Western media that had previously championed the cause of freedom-seeking Iranian students and clerics now stood by, mute, as revolutionaries trampled on individual rights. To be sure, the same press had played into Khomeini's hands before. In November 1978 Iran's prison population was only 300—in a nation of 35 million people —but much of the Western press had uncritically accepted

Khomeini's fabricated figure of a staggering 300,000.

President Carter, who had received low ratings for foreign policy in his first year in office, now saw his overall ratings plummet. In March 1979, even after his successful peacemaking trip to the Middle East, only 29 percent of respondents to one poll approved his presidency. While most of the dissatisfaction related to his handling of the economy, less than half of those polled (44 percent) endorsed the direction of his foreign policy. By early summer the numbers had dipped further: only 13 percent believed that the nation's position in the world was "growing stronger," while 62 percent believed it was "becoming weaker." [25]

Events in Iran reached a nadir with the seizure by militant students of 66 American hostages at the U.S. embassy on November 4, 1979. As they had in a similar attack nine months earlier, which lasted only a day, the militants fearlessly overran the ill-secured embassy. The hostages would be held captive for an agonizing 14 months.

The Carter administration's inability to understand Khomeini and his ambitions led inexorably to the formation of the Islamic Republic of Iran, under which the ayatollah exercised unlimited power.

Through these four stages, which spanned nearly the entire Carter presidency, Washington failed to act effectively to prevent militant Islam from gaining a foothold in the Persian Gulf region that it would expand around the world, yielding dire consequences that reverberate years after September 11, 2001.

Following his flight into exile, the shah was asked what would happen if the country's Islamic mullahs were to lead a revolution and seize Iran's government. "They would take us back 1,500 years," he answered ruefully. "They would put the women back under the veil. Before the revolution, the women were in the category of the fools—the crazy people. They had no rights—no right to vote, no right to express themselves."[26]

This and other elements of the shah's gloomy prophecy were indeed fulfilled, and Iran's women were far from the sole victims of the theocratic revolution that replaced the long-standing monarchy. The shah had hoped for his friend Gerald Ford to win the election, and Carter's ascent to the presidency in 1977 was a blow to the monarchy. Carter, the shah thought, might resemble John Kennedy, whom the shah had disliked, in part because of the pressure Kennedy applied for the shah to reform his political system. Now Carter's frequently emphasized goals of human rights and arms reductions might cause a rupture in the kind of relationships Iran had enjoyed with Richard Nixon and Ford. [27]

In his inaugural address on January 20, 1977, Carter signaled the coming change, stating: "Our moral sense dictates a clear preference for those societies which share with us an abiding respect for individual human rights."[28] In time, Iran's ambassador in Washington, Ardeshir Zahedi, expressed concerns in private conversations that presidential human rights slogans were likely to cause confusion and disarray in Iran. He thought that a call for human rights could easily be interpreted as American disapproval of the shah's domestic policies and an encouragement to the opposition.

Within the administration, National Security Adviser Zbigniew Brzezinski noted that offers of help to the shah were often laden with preconditions. "Personally and through the State Department," he wrote, "I continued to express my support for the shah, but at the same time we were pressing him to act forcefully on his own to resolve with his political opponents as many disputes as possible." He added: "The shah was never explicitly urged to be tough; U.S. assurances of support were watered down by simultaneous reminders of the need to do more about progress toward genuine democracy; coalition with the opposition was mentioned always as a desirable objective." [29]

Robert Armao, a public relations official and a close friend of the shah's who traveled with him in exile during his last years, once observed, "That decision [the Carter administration's failure to support the shah] will turn out to be one of the worst ones the United States ever made." Given the spread of militant Islamic fundamentalism a quarter of a century later, who can argue?

Through the late 1970s the fortunes of Islamic fundamentalism rose exponentially. Something could have been done, but wasn't, to impede the growth of the movement. The consequences of having withheld needed support from the shah of Iran and from the fragile secular government that remained, briefly, after his departure—not to mention the Carter's administration's equivocation about admitting the shah to the United States, at least for urgently needed medical treatment, when he was forced to flee his homeland—are incalculable.

Throughout the Iran crisis—from the impending revolution, to the shah's exile, to the seizure of American hostages in the takeover of the U.S. embassy in Tehran—President Jimmy Carter was forever reactive, never proactive. One author cites Carter's response to the Iran crisis as a prime example of his shortcomings as a leader. He faults the Carter administration for being "slow to respond to the mounting crisis, sometimes even seeming oblivious" to the course of events in Iran.[30] The White House thus failed miserably to provide clear leadership when it was most sorely needed.

In the fall of 1978, as the horizon grew darker for the shah, Carter had two realistic policy options: to support the shah against the rising tide of revolutionary sentiment, a position favored by his National Security Council; or to work toward the formation of some kind of coalition government, which would necessarily include followers of Khomeini, an option advocated by the State Department. Given those options, "Carter chose instead to waffle," in the words of one observer. [31]

The Iranian revolution's ultimate goal was to transform the world along Islamic lines. The wearing of the veil and full Islamic dress was made compulsory for women in April 1983, soon after the last of Iran's leftist movements had been crushed by the ruling party. Members of the party's powerful committees hunted down and prosecuted ill-veiled women according to strict criteria for garment lengths, shapes, and colors that today remain in force and are still posted in all public places in Iran.

The revolution demonstrated that a populist Islamic movement could bring down a powerful government, even one closely connected to the United States. The example of the Khomeini-led Iranian revolution convinced many observers that Islam had supplanted nationalism as the principal factor in the political, social, and cultural identity of certain countries.

* * *

The war against radical Islam is *the* battle royal, now and for the foreseeable future. With the Cold War long past, we are faced with an incalculably furtive opponent, one less predictable and thus far more fearsome than the Soviet Union. This opponent is tribal and therefore transnational, loyal only to its religious fervor. Anyone lacking that fervor—including fellow Muslims—is viewed by radical Islamists as barbaric and, therefore, a deserving target of their righteous fury. This opponent's strikes can never be anticipated, nor are its actions ever as measured or comprehensible as were the Soviets'.

To make the case that it was the United States' desertion of the shah that resulted in the fall of Iran and the ensuing warp-speed growth of radical Islam, we need to look at the complete picture. Thus it is my aim in this book to bring into sharp focus the picture of Islamic fundamentalism both before and after the Iranian revolution. I will bolster my central argument: the Carter administration's crucial failure to support the faltering shah of Iran opened a Pandora's box that can never be sealed.

It is safe to say that Carter was for the most part occupied with the Cold War rivalry with the Soviet Union. The Carter administration, and Reagan administration to follow, did not shift focus away from the Soviet Union, largely perceiving the new Islamists as a mere nuisance rather than a serious threat. The December 1979 Soviet invasion of Afghanistan reminded U.S. decision makers that the strategic clash with the Communist camp was of a higher order than a confrontation with the new Islamist challenge emerging from Tehran. The latter paled in comparison with the Cold War rivalry that had preoccupied the United States since the later 1940s. Carter wrote in his diary that the Soviet invasion of Afghanistan was "the most serious international development that has occurred since I have been President." The implications of the Soviet move, added Carter, "could pose the most serious threat to the peace since the Second World War." [32]

But this was hyperbole born of presidential license. Despite the convulsions of the Islamic revolutions in Iran and its global impact in several Muslim states, the Carter administration did not enunciate a policy statement, let alone a full-fledged policy, toward political Islam. To U.S. officials, Islamic resurgence was but a temporary distraction from the Cold War. American foreign policy still revolved around the containment of Soviet Communism, not Islamism.

In reality, writes Fawaz Gerges,

> Iran's impact was more than academic. It has had a "profound effect" on the formulation and conduct of U.S. policy toward the larger Middle East ever since. In the American mind, populist, revolutionary Islam came to be associated with terrorism and the promotion of subversive activities. Domestically, Carter's inability to respond to effectively to the Islamic Republic of Iran—let alone to free the hostages there—coupled with his failure to communicate his policy on Iran and on the hostages in particular to the American public, became one of the main rocks on which the presidential reelection bid crashed. [33]

Despite these policy failures, this book does not seek to cast aspersions on Jimmy Carter's character. Carter was and is a person of strong moral fiber—a World War II veteran and a person of unquestioned integrity. He and his wife, Rosalynn, are committed leaders in Habitat for Humanity, a charitable organization that builds housing for the poor. In April 1990, *Newsweek* called Carter "the modern model of a successful ex-president of the United States." The following month he was awarded the Liberty Medal and a $100,000 prize for his involvement in "issues of liberty around the world."[34] Not only was the Panama Canal treaty ratified, in June 1979 he signed the SALT II Treaty with the Soviet Union at the Vienna Summit. Nevertheless, he led an administration whose foreign policy had catastrophic consequences in Iran.

Before the time of the Islamic revolution, 25 years ago, which gave birth to the Islamic state of Iran, the battle against Islamic extremism had yet to be joined. Radical Islam was then, as it had been for decades before, an impassioned ideology espoused by a relative handful of activists across the Middle East. Ideology had not yet been translated into subversive practice. Religious philosophy only occasionally was the cause of armed conflict.

Militant fundamentalism had first appeared a half-century earlier, around the emergence of the Muslim Brotherhood (also known as the Muslim Brothers or Brethren) in Egypt and other Middle Eastern countries, as discussed in Chapter 1. But radical Islam gained substantial ground with Khomeini's seizure of power in Iran; it now had both a base and, as the working government of a sovereign state, legitimacy. Chapter 2 explains how the Carter administration's failure to support Iran when the shah's regime was imperiled led inevitably to the establishment of the Islamic Republic, with its pretense of lawfulness inscribed in a constitution.

"In most Islamic countries, revolutionary Iran's influence has been indirect, with Iran serving primarily as exemplar rather than direct participant," writes historian John Esposito. And the influence of the revolution in Iran didn't merely extend to other Shiites. "Sunnis and Shia across the Islamic world were applauding the courage and faith of the revolutionaries, and Iran was equated with Islamic revivalism and fundamentalism," Esposito continues. "Iran's example served as a catalyst to local Muslim activists whose own grievances now seemed neither unique nor insurmountable."[35]

The revolution's success led to political outbursts in such diverse places as Saudi Arabia, Pakistan, Kuwait, and Bahrain. Representatives of Muslim organizations from the Middle East and South and Southeast Asia traveled to Tehran immediately after the revolution.

Arguably, the most pervasive way in which revolutionary Iran has influenced the Muslim world is on the level of ideas and ideology. Characteristic of the Islamic revival has been the worldwide dissemination of the ideas of such Sunni ideologues as the Egyptians Hasan al-Banna and Sayyid Qutb, the Pakistani Abul Ala Mawdudi, and the Indian Abul Hasan Ali Nadvi. As a result of the revolution, the writings of Khomeini and Ali Shariati have been widely translated and distributed throughout the Muslim (and indeed the non-Muslim) world. Whether or not there is a direct connection between ideas and oppositional activity, it is certainly true that the post-revolutionary generation of Muslims across the world accepts that Islam provides a blueprint for political and social reform.

Radical Islam thus became a full-blown political

entity. Although anchored in a religious creed, this phenomenon—sometimes referred to as "extremist Islam," "militant Islam," or, simply, "Islamism"—now represents a radical utopian movement that is far closer in spirit to forms of totalitarianism such as fascism, falangism, and communism than to traditional religion. It often expresses itself through the deadliest language of our time—terrorism—whether it is doing battle against a secular regime in its home countries or against Western nations.

How could President Carter and his administration have allowed this disaster to occur? This book will shed new light on that pivotal question. Carter's Iran policy was at once inscrutable and contradictory. His administration was invariably, and fatally, slow to react as events during the crisis transpired at a feverish pace. In the end, it seemed that this divided, dilatory American government effectively had no Iran policy whatsoever.

* * *

Former U.S. Attorney General Ramsey Clark, for example, reportedly remains proud of his anti-shah crusade of 1979. In a recent interview he described the shah's overthrow as "the accomplishment of his lifetime," citing exaggerated numbers of the shah's victims as the moral justification for his crusade.

In the first interview granted after his flight to exile in 1979, the shah expressed his consternation with exaggerated reports of his regime's brutality to the journalist David Frost.

Frost: The terrorists—the Khomeinists—their charges have been wide-ranging. What about the charge that you have killed more than 100,000 people?

Shah: In my regime—100,000 people? On what occasion? It is preposterous.

Frost: We cannot substantiate it.

Shah: They don't even know how to count.

Frost: Even your worst critics, if you put together all the people killed in shootouts or shootouts up until the middle of 1977, it would be about 1,500.

Shah: Not even that. It's certainly below 1,000.

Frost: Then of course there are the riots in the last year, and the figures he quotes here are enormous. Would you say that during the riots 10,000 people died?

Shah: No, never. Never in the world. First of all, who are they? People committing arson in storehouses and hotels, libraries—in no country in the world would you just stand by and look at this.

Frost: We have been talking about the difference between the Ayatollah's figures and your figures, and yours are much lower than his.

Shah: They say anything; they say 1,000, then 10,000, then 100,000. We've never had more than 3,200 political prisoners, most of them terrorists. And even an international organization like Amnesty International talks about 10,000, 20,000, 100,000 prisoners. I mean, absolutely irresponsible figures. [36]

* * *

Chapter 4 addresses the establishment of another militant Islamic base, in Afghanistan. A month after the hostages had been seized at the U.S. embassy in Tehran in November 1979, the Soviet Army invaded Afghanistan to assist that country's beleaguered communist government, which was battling a loose coalition of *mujahidin*, or Islamic freedom fighters. In the context of the Cold War, the United States viewed the Soviet invasion as an intolerable threat to the regional balance of power. The American government threw its support to the mujahidin resistance.

The Red Army's invasion suddenly thrust the majority of Afghans into the ranks of the resistance, which saw itself as an offshoot and outgrowth of ordinary Muslim society. It rode a wave of popular approval not unlike the one Khomeini had enjoyed, with his exaltation of the "Islam of the people." The mujahidin received aid, military and otherwise, from Saudi Arabia, Iran, and Pakistan, as well as the United States. The mujahidin were perceived by the West as anticommunist warriors and by the Saudis as the vanguard of the great jihad. By 1982 the mujahidin forces were receiving $600 million per year in U.S. aid and a matching amount from Saudi Arabia. This was a well-funded war of resistance. Indeed, the Saudi dollar-for-dollar match with the U.S. taxpayer was fundamental to the success of the ten-year engagement in Afghanistan. The net effect was to create a kind of camp for terrorists in Afghanistan, with historic and disastrous consequences for the region and the world that lasted until the overthrow of the Taliban regime.

Beyond dispute were the immediate and long-term effects of the Iranian revolution. The revolution was clearly a setback for the United States' interests in the area. The fall of the shah left the Gulf without a reliable partner in the area. Iran was now venomously anti-American, referring to Washington as the "Big Satan."

In addition, the fall of the shah inspired extremists around the world. The exile of the American-supported shah and the subsequent revolution were proof positive that militants could unseat a secular, Western-backed government and install a radical Islamic state. Further, the rise of international terrorism has had a profound impact on world change.

In the 1970s the confirmed number of terrorist incidents worldwide was 8,114. The toll was 4,978 people killed and 6,902 injured. But the terror toll of the 1980s trumped the 1970s many times over. The decade produced some 31,426 confirmed incidents of terror, with 70,589 killed and 47,849 injured. [37]

With respect to the fortunes of militant Islam, the Iranian revolution acted as the grandfather of political Islam for the next 25 years.

In a divided Carter administration, Secretary of State Cyrus Vance advocated liberalization and political reform in Iran over aggressive support for the shah.

The global spread of Islamic fundamentalism and its stepchild, terrorism, is evident in a display of Osama bin Laden's image in the streets of Kuala Lumpur, Malaysia.

Jimmy Carter's presidency was full of promise on his first day in office in January 1977, but his tenure, marred by the mismanaged Iran crisis, would be limited to a single term.

Mujahidin gathered in Afghanistan's capital, Kabul, in May 1992, a month after the country's last Soviet-installed president, Ahmadzai Najibullah, resigned.

A week after the September 11, 2001, terrorist attacks in New York and Washington, demonstrators in Karachi, Pakistan, proclaimed Osama bin Laden their hero.

Afghan mujahidin paused during a February 1987 attack against a Soviet military post in Amatal. The Soviet Union ended its 10-year occupation of Afghanistan in 1989.

Vestiges of communism, such as a bust of Lenin, were destroyed by Afghan freedom fighters following the 1992 ouster of the Soviet-sponsored Najibullah government.

Carter's national security adviser, Zbigniew Brzezinski, urged the president to support the shah in order to protect U.S. strategic interests in the Persian Gulf region.

Chapter 1

Radical Islam before the
Revolution in Iran

Anyone looking at the world in 2007 is entitled to ask, "How did we get here?" What chain of causes has led to the acts of militant Islam that we have observed and the ever-present sense of impending disaster that we feel? How did we arrive at a point at which the World Trade Center was bombed twice? How has it come to pass that hostages from different nations are beheaded, with the grisly scenes captured on websites, while the reaction of many is indifference because the action is regarded as commonplace?

Less than ten years into the new millennium, millions of people live in a state of steady, low-boil anxiety. They are waiting for something bad to happen. They are afraid to fly, loathe traveling to unfamiliar places, and fear even the most ordinary kinds of excursions, like riding their morning commuter train from the suburbs or entering the New York City subway. Meanwhile, members of the National Guard patrol our great public spaces.

The effect of this omnipresent fear of terrorism is that our freedom is circumscribed and our economy weakened. One professional man in New York wonders when the next attack is coming and worries about the safety of his wife, who works at the United Nations. A woman who worked in the World Trade Center can no longer bring herself to enter a high-rise building. Americans everywhere have lost confidence in the ability of their government to protect them. Indeed, the recent September 11 Commission hearings only exacerbated the sense that our leaders are exquisitely, and sadly, fragile.

How did we get to this point?

There was a time when Islamic fundamentalism didn't entail militant action. In the years before the Iranian revolution in 1979, fundamentalism bore a more benign face. For decades it existed as little more than a fringe phenomenon, far removed from the worldwide impact it now exerts. All that changed with the revolution in Iran. The revolution gave radical Islam a legitimacy it had previously lacked. It also provided a base of operations for militants to come. The revolution utterly changed the political fortunes of Islam and, by extension, of the West. Nearly every nation, Western, Arab, and otherwise, would be significantly affected by the event and its aftermath.

The revolution wasn't bound to succeed, but it did. Our leaders, a quarter-century ago and earlier, failed to act in a way that would have altered the course of history. But that is the second part of my argument, in which I will show how the Carter administration failed in four different stages of the Iran crisis. I will hold that argument in abeyance until Chapters 2 and 3. At this point I want to demonstrate, albeit briefly, that from the 1920s through

the 1970s, Islamic fundamentalism would become progressively more *ideological* and *politically active*. In the last 25
years political Islam has ascended a staircase of greater and
greater intolerance, coupled with increasing violence. This
transformation began with an innocent-sounding organization called the Muslim Brotherhood.

* * *

Organized militant Islamic groups existed as far back
as 1928. The early groups were spirited organizations, dis-
seminating ideas that challenged the colonialism of the
French and British; philosophically, they were anti-Western and contemptuous of Arab leaders they considered
puppets of the West. Despite their presence as a flashpoint
for dissent within their societies and governments, they
lacked a consistent practical philosophy and did not advocate the use of violence as a means to achieving their ends.

A look at the lives and thinking of two of these leaders
demonstrates that harsh words did not initially result in
militant deeds.

Hasan al-Banna and the Birth of the Muslim Brotherhood

The nucleus of the Muslim Brotherhood was formed
in Egypt in the late 1920s. The organization's founder was
Hasan al-Banna (1906–1949), a 22-year-old teacher. In time
the young teacher founded what he called a "Brotherhood
in the service of Islam." It exists to this day. He promised
for Egypt a return to the caliphate, or Islamic leadership,
which would govern according to the *sharia* (Islamic law).
Al-Banna, a strident antisecularist, sought to link the

flowering of Islam to anticolonialism. Moreover, he rejected the more benign interpretation of *jihad* prescribed by the Muslim *ulama* (religious scholars). Jihad in their view was internal, denoting a struggle against one's own bad habits or irreligious behavior. Jihad can also denote a war ordained in the service of religion, however, and it was this interpretation that al-Banna embraced and expounded, i.e., that all Muslims have an unceasing duty to wage war on Islam's behalf.

He held to a fundamental conviction that Islam does not accept—or really even tolerate—a separation of "church" and state. His enduring aim was the creation of an Islamic state, following the example of Muhammad's establishment of the Medinese state, the first such Islamic entity. Al-Banna believed an Islamic state would draw Muslims to the overriding mission of restoring the original "community of believers" of Muhammad's time in the seventh century and bringing the rest of the world, the unbelievers, under the influence of God's law and His true religion.

It was al-Banna's uncompromising philosophy—and the economic and religious discontent stirring among his followers—that gave the movement its thrust. Egypt's leaders were establishment figures who had abandoned any vision of an Islamic state. That was exactly what al-Banna proposed: a state modeled on the Prophet's Era. Such a state would be created, he said, by expelling the British and then purging Egypt of all non-Islamic influence. He reminded his followers that Islam offered all that they needed, now and forever. It was "all-inclusive, encompassing the affairs of people in this world and the hereafter . . . an ideology and a ritual, a home and a nationality, a religion and a state, a spirit and work, a book and a sword."[1]

Such a sweeping worldview left no room for the uncommitted, and the "sword," if needed, would play a prominent role in the jihad of which he spoke. As one historian noted, "Al-Banna's genius lay in comforting the needy of all classes with a promise of Islamic resurrection."[2] He was a gifted orator. One of al-Banna's disciples wrote, "His mastery over his followers was complete and inclusive, almost approaching sorcery," while another follower spoke of "the spiritual bond between himself and his listeners."[3]

In 1948 a more strident Brotherhood attempted to overthrow the Egyptian state. Police forces responded, but not before the Brothers had assassinated public officials, including the prime minister. Six weeks later, on February 12, 1949, Hasan al-Banna, esteemed by his Muslim Brethren as an *imam*, or a leader "worthy of emulation," was gunned down by assassins as he exited the Young Men's Muslim Association headquarters in Cairo. His assailants were members of the government's secret police. They were eventually brought to trial, but only after a new, revolutionary government reopened the case in 1952. In 1954 four convicted assailants were sentenced to prison terms ranging from one year to life.

So charismatic a leader had al-Banna been that after his death the membership of the Brethren declined precipitously. Hasan al-Hudaybi, the elderly judge who succeeded him, was regarded as lackluster in comparison. The Brotherhood had lost its founder and inspirational leader, but its influence on the future of Islamic radicalism would be significant.

Sayyid Qutb: *Jahiliyya* and Violence

Not long after al-Banna's assassination, the head of the Brotherhood's women's division, Zainab al-Ghazzali,

encouraged Sayyid Qutb to assume the long-term leadership of the movement. Qutb, a disciple of al-Banna, was
already a leading spokesman for the Brotherhood and the
editor of its journal. "In the world there is only one party
of God, all others are parties of Satan and rebellion,"
Qutb wrote portentously in "A Muslim's Nationality." He
continued, "Those who believe fight in the cause of God,
and those who disbelieve fight in the cause of rebellion."[4]

Qutb soon became the chief ideologue of the Muslim
Brotherhood. Little in this onetime literature major's background suggested that he would promulgate radical con-
cepts that would endure long after his death, providing the
philosophical underpinnings for some of the most violent
terrorist acts of modern history—including those committed by Osama bin Laden and Ayman al-Zawahiri—but
that is in fact what happened. Qutb's ideas would be cited
by Anwar Sadat's assassins in 1981. Even before then, bin
Laden was avidly imbibing Qutb's philosophy. [5]

Qutb was the father of modern fundamentalism. Under
Qutb's leadership the Brotherhood readily employed violence in the pursuit of its over-arching goal: the creation of
an Islamic state. Qutb taught that the Prophet Muhammad's holy war to end *jahiliyya*—the era of "ignorance"
and barbarism in Arabia that preceded the arrival of Islam
—had succeeded 13 centuries earlier.

Jahiliyya became the rallying cry for those who shared
Qutb's determined vision. In characterizing irreligious
regimes he frequently invoked this ancient Islamic concept. Harking back to the condition of the world before
the Koranic revelation in the seventh century, Qutb urged
that governments be overhauled according to Islamic
precepts. His preoccupation with jahiliyya was far from

merely theoretical; it was pragmatic, a way to describe a program to be enacted.

In October 1954 an attempt was made on the life of Egyptian President Gamal Abdel Nasser. The attempt provided him a reason to round up and arrest thousands of members of the Muslim Brotherhood, which he had previously dissolved as an opposition political party. Qutb was among those arrested. Seven leading members of the Brotherhood were sentenced to death. One received a sentence of life in prison, but the other six were hanged. Qutb was sentenced to 15 years in prison. The Brotherhood was forced underground.

Now Qutb's views were colored by the harshness of captivity. He witnessed the slaughter of 23 imprisoned members of the Brotherhood in 1957, when prison officials opened fire on detainees who had staged a sit-in and refused to work in quarries. Qutb himself suffered torture and concluded that Nasser and his followers would wield power solely to serve their own interests, and that the interests of their secular Egyptian society would always be antithetical to those of Islam.

A simmering advocacy of revolution came to characterize Qutb's writings. He recommended the replacement of any authoritarian or secular jahilli state by an Islamic order based on sharia. Qutb realized that such a task was ambitious and would take a long time to achieve. Much ideological and organizational work had to be done, and only a trained and dedicated coterie of true believers— who would resort to force when threatened—could preside over the new Islamic order. The task was further complicated by the current prevalence of Western ideas. The allure of such ideas was more seductive than at any other time in the history of Islam, Qutb believed. In Egypt and elsewhere, secular elites had emerged, nationalism had weakened religious solidarity, and the Islamic establishment had grown increasingly subservient to government and isolated from everyday life.

During his imprisonment Qutb carried on a clandestine correspondence with some 250 Brotherhood militants, who adopted his views on Arab and Western societies—expressed in *In the Shade of the Koran* and *Milestones*—and would spread them further. Qutb was released from prison in December 1964, but was rearrested in August 1965. Two weeks later his sisters Amina and Hamida were also arrested, along with the leading female member of the Brotherhood, Zaynab al-Ghazali. Qutb was accused of subversion, terrorism, and encouraging sedition.

The charge of subversion stemmed from Qutb's appointment by Hasan Hudaybi (who had succeeded the Brotherhood's founder and original leader, al-Banna) to organize Brotherhood chapters in the jails and prison camps of Egypt. The resulting organization, known as the Tanzim, was allegedly dedicated to the violent overthrow of the Egyptian government, although no evidence established that Qutb, or any group under his influence, had plotted armed insurrection.

The sedition charge was attributable mainly to the immensely popular *Milestones*, which had undergone six printings in the first six months of 1965. With its broad appeal and revolutionary implications, the book worried Egyptian authorities. Qutb had written forcefully about the need to replace secular values and systems with genuine Islamic counterparts and espoused the following views:

It is essential for mankind to have new leadership!

The leadership of mankind by Western man is now on the decline, not because Western culture has become poor materially or because its economic and military power has become weak.

The period of the Western system has come to an end primarily because it is deprived of those life-giving values which enabled it to be the leader of mankind.

It is necessary for the new leadership to preserve and develop the material fruits of the creative genius of Europe, and also to provide mankind with such high ideals and values as have so far remained undiscovered by mankind, and which will also acquaint humanity with a way of life which is harmonious with human nature.

Islam is the only system which possesses these values and this way of life.[6]

On May 17, 1966, an Egyptian court condemned Qutb and six other prominent members of the Brotherhood to death. Four of those sentences were commuted to life imprisonment, but Qutb was hanged in Cairo on August 29, 1966. His legacy would include a philosophy that was interpreted and adopted by generations of future radical Islamists. *Milestones* would be cited to justify the overthrow not only of oppressive governments, but of secular regimes of any kind, repressive or not. In Qutb's view, any society that did not adhere to the directives of the Koran, the *hadith* (the lessons of the Prophet) and sharia existed in a state of complete ignorance. The power of his writings was such that anyone who owned a copy of *Milestones* could be arrested and charged with sedition.[7]

Muslims must emulate the life of the Prophet, he said, and not shrink from the use of force, if necessary, in order to establish a Muslim state. Qutb's extreme views were not universally endorsed within the Muslim Brotherhood. Some elements of the organization rejected his radicalism. The depth and sincerity of a Muslim's faith should be judged only by Allah, not by radical theologians, they maintained. These members of the Brotherhood called for the education, rather than the coercion, of the Muslim masses. They did not participate in the declaration of a state of jahiliyya. Although they were no more optimistic than the radicals about the prevailing political and social climate, they dismissed the tactic of employing violence to form a new government.

Inside Egypt, Qutb's legacy included the appearance of a new breed of radical activist, unaffiliated with the Muslim Brotherhood. Among this new generation were Abd al-Salam Faraj, the author of *The Neglected Duty*, and Sheikh Omar Abdel-Rahman, the mentor of the Islamic Societies.

Qutb was a seminal Islamic thinker, whose teachings would furnish an intellectual rationale for the actions of radicals such as Sheikh Omar, who was convicted of plotting to bomb the World Trade Center and other New York City structures in 1993. Despite his probable involvement, he was acquitted of playing a role in the assassination of

Egyptian President Anwar Sadat in October 1981.

The militant ideas and exhortations expressed in the speeches and writings of Hasan Al-Banna and Sayyid Qutb did not precipitate sustained violence during their lifetimes. These thinkers laid the ideological groundwork for militant Islam, but their ideas were not translated into everyday practice. Even had they planned to launch an extensive campaign of militancy, both would have found the surrounding political milieu too repressive to wage a violent rebellion for very long.

In order for militant Islam to take a more permanent hold, it required a base of operations. That base was formed when the shah of Iran was forced into exile and an Islamic government was established in Iran, a country that historically was one of the most tolerant in the Middle East.

Chapter 2

Jimmy Carter and the Reign of the Shah

In 1953—25 years before the shah would contemplate his final flight into exile, while the long-banished Ayatollah Khomeini prepared to return to Iran—the shah faced a crisis. With his rule threatened, his relationship with the United States would prove crucial in extricating him from his troubles. A quarter of a century later, he found himself in crisis again. This time he would need the support of a new American president, Jimmy Carter. Before examining the connection between the Carter administration and Iran, it is important to consider the shah's relationships with previous American presidents.

* * *

Mohammed Reza Pahlavi, the shah of Iran, confronted the first major challenge of his 12-year reign in 1953. Prime Minister Mohammed Mossadeq, the hero of the nationalist opposition, threatened to usurp the shah's rule. Another prime minister—Great Britain's Winston Churchill—urged Iran's monarch to take decisive action. Wiring the shah, he wrote:

> I should be glad if Mr. Henderson [the United States ambassador to Iran] would transmit to the shah the following observation of a general character which I believe is correct and in accordance with democratic principles. It is the duty of a constitutional monarch or President when faced with violent tyrannical action by individuals or a minority party to take the necessary steps to secure the well-being of the toiling masses and the continuity of an ordered state. [1]

To the shah the message conveyed yet another assurance, like those he had received in the 1940s from President Franklin Roosevelt—who was convinced that a strong Iran was in America's best interests—that his well-being lay in following the advice of the United States and Great Britain.

With the help of these two countries, the shah weathered the 1953 crisis. In a coup supported by the CIA, Mossadeq's nationalist government was overthrown and the shah returned to power. The shah would rule Iran for another quarter-century, during which time he would introduce an array of reforms aimed at placating both his subjects and his Western allies, especially the United States. But in the late 1970s, as protests and riots threatened his regime, the shah had no Churchill or Roosevelt to support and guide him. He waited for Washington to formulate a firm policy and plan of action. He waited in vain.

* * *

At its inception, in 1941, the shah's reign began inauspiciously. Having expelled the Germans from Iran in July of that year, British and Russian forces invaded the country in August.

The shah's father, Reza Shah Pahlavi, had abdicated the so-called Peacock Throne, telling his son, "I cannot be the nominal head of an occupied land, to be dictated to by a minor English or Russian officer." He died three years later, after the British had appointed his son as his successor.

Living up to the legacy of the father was no small task. Emulating the Turkish leader Mustafa Kemal Ataturk, the elder Pahlavi had implemented reforms similar to those that Ataturk had introduced in Turkey. The first ten years of his rule had brought greater progress to Iran than had occurred in the entire Qajar period of the previous 120 years. Reza Shah built roads, schools, and hospitals and sent students abroad for further education. He developed textile, sugar, and cement industries, introduced electrification, and embarked on the construction of a vastly ambitious railroad across the country, linking the Persian Gulf to the Caspian Sea. His Western-style reforms alienated Shiite religious officials, however, whose influence declined as a result of them.

Reza Shah's son was not only young, but also inexperienced, when he assumed the throne. (The British would form an impression of him as a weak-willed philanderer; he was twice divorced by 1958). But his recognition of the importance of fostering a strong alliance with the United States hinted at an instinct for statecraft. For its part, the

U.S. State Department demonstrated its interest in the 25-year-old shah's fortunes when it advised President Roosevelt that postwar Iran should be strengthened in order to resist encroachments by Britain and Russia. The notion appealed to Roosevelt, who wrote a celebrated memorandum to Cordell Hull, the secretary of state, in which he declared that he was "thrilled by the idea of using Iran as an example of what we could do by an unselfish American policy. We could not take on a more difficult nation than Iran. I should like, however, to have a try at it."[2]

In 1949 the shah narrowly escaped the first of three attempts on his life. The attacker was a young man who appeared to be aligned with both the communist-controlled *Tudeh* (People's) Party and what the shah called "archconservative religious fanatics." The monarch declared martial law and had the communists arrested. It was appropriate that his attacker would represent the two allegiances—secular and religious—that together would drive the shah from his throne 30 years later.

The shah's rule underwent a stern test in 1953, when a coalition of parties headed by Mossadeq demonstrated what a powerful force nationalism could be. The nationalists' main targets were Britain and the Anglo-Iranian Oil Company. Mossadeq and his followers in the Majlis, or parliament, insisted on Iran's right to regain control over its principal natural resource. So aroused was public opinion that by May 1951 the young shah was forced to appoint Mossadeq prime minister and give his assent to a bill nationalizing the Iranian oil industry. Not only was the measure welcomed in Iran; it inspired the Arab man-in-the-street elsewhere in the region. While by mid-1952 Mossadeq's popularity had waned among Iran's middle class, his nationalist fervor maintained wide appeal among the poor and the clergy, and throughout the Middle East he enjoyed a stature comparable to that of Nasser in Egypt a few years later.

As doubts about his leadership grew among Iranian politicians, the emboldened shah attempted to replace Mossadeq with a loyalist general as prime minister. But the shah's maneuver failed, and he was forced to flee the country briefly in August 1953. A mere six days later he returned, in time to witness Mossadeq's overthrow by a counter-coup organized by the CIA, with substantial assistance from British intelligence. U.S. Army forces, aided by the CIA, restored the shah to power, but the intrusive operation incited in many Iranian quarters, secular as well as religious, loathing and distrust of the United States. Mossadeq's public trial, in December 1953, enhanced his popularity, especially among Islamic clerics.

Iran's tattered relations with Britain were repaired, but it was the United States that now reigned as the principal Western influence in the country. As a result of the shah's ensuing program of reforms, Iran came to exemplify Western-style progress and development. The shah also took care to mute his opposition. Elections to the Majlis were carefully controlled in order to guarantee the desired outcome. The National Front ceased to function as an organized political force, and the communist Tudeh Party was outlawed. Power was increasingly concentrated in the hands of the shah.

By the early 1960s, however, the Kennedy administration had grown unhappy with the pace of reform in Iran. A State Department cable reminded Tehran that reforms were necessary "because it is generally agreed that without some reforms Iran was likely, as Khrushchev predicted, to fall to the Soviets like a ripe plum." In addition, a 1961 Presidential Task Force on Iran noted that "the shah is a highly complex personality: intelligent and forceful on occasion, but often moody, erratic, and indecisive. He is constantly haunted by the fear that the United States might abandon him for one reason or another and has been particularly uneasy over the new United States Administration's attitude toward him."[3]

As always, unfettered access to American weapons was the shah's principal concern. Fearing that Iran was a mere relationship of convenience for the United States, he worried that he could be discarded at any time. A succession of U.S. presidents deemed the relationship strategically important and prized him as an ally, but the Task Force analysis was nevertheless accurate. His fortunes were inextricably bound up with those of the United States, and thus depended on the support of the current occupant of the White House.

In April 1962 the shah came to Washington. During his visit he related to Kennedy his officers' concerns that U.S. military aid to Iran was inadequate. Kennedy's rejoinder was that Iran's main problems lay with Iran, not the United States; internal changes were necessary. The shah acknowledged the need for reforms, but insisted that what his country needed most was "an honest first-class army with a decent standard of living." He explained that such an army could rebuff communist threats while providing the stability required to transform Iran into a model of cooperation with the United States. Kennedy concurred. "There are always special factors that have to be taken into account in different countries," JFK observed. "We are aware that the shah is the keystone to the arch in Iran."[4]

The shah was determined to show that he was a for-ward-thinking leader. "I am not content with seeing Iran as a progressive country," he said. "I want my country to be a model country, a model of justice and the administration of justice and a model of progress. We have the possibili-ties for making Iran a model country." He believed that Iran was on the verge of a radical social and political trans-formation that would allow it to "catch up" with the West. His plans were in place. Many of the progressive programs that he would launch in the 1960s and '70s—including the major reforms known collectively as the White Revolution (so called because it was meant to be bloodless)—had been formulated during the 1950s.

The separate points of his White Revolution included land reform, nationalization of the forests, profit sharing for industrial workers, the sale of state factories, voting rights for women, and the establishment of a Literacy Corps. The United States was pleased. A message of congratula-tions from Kennedy followed the shah's announcement of the sweeping measures.

But the shah faced domestic opposition. Some Irani-ans were dubious about putting power in the hands of "ig-norant countrymen and industrial workers." The shah nevertheless pursued, and even intensified, some of the reform measures. Land reform was extended to include certain Islamic properties (whose revenues had been ap-plied to the upkeep of mosques or to charitable works), while the holdings of large landowners would now be lim-ited to a single village. Not only was female suffrage intro-duced, but other women's rights were legally strengthened. Through the Literacy Corps, high school students were permitted to teach in village schools as an alternative to military service.

Sounding a counterpoint to these reforms were the views of his opponents. The National Front declared that the reforms were unconstitutional. The mullahs—whose effective spokesman was a vociferous cleric, Ayatollah Ruhollah Khomeini, from the holy city of Qum—denounced the measures as "un-Islamic" as well as unconstitutional. The White Revolution met grass roots–level resistance from Muslim clerics, many of whom, like rich private landlords, owned vast estates.

Landlords, clerics, and other opponents encouraged protests that took place in Qum at the end of 1962 and more serious riots that erupted in Tehran in June 1963. Estimates of casualties varied, with the government claiming no more than several hundred, while eyewitnesses put the figure at closer to several thousand. Whatever the total might actually have been, the clashes marked the beginning of a prolonged uprising against the shah's rule.

The shah endured constant criticism from the senior ulama. Privately, he believed that the mullahs should be barred from participation in politics, but he sensed that the time was not yet ripe to effect such a change. An observer remarked that the shah's father "must have been spinning in his grave to see the growing arrogance and effrontery of the mullahs rampant in the holy city. How the old tyrant must despise the weakness of his son, who has allowed these turbulent priests to regain so much of their reactionary influence."

Despite the attacks from the clerics, the White Revolution achieved abundant success. Property was distributed to landless peasants, the literacy rate increased, industrialization proceeded apace, women gained unprecedented freedom, and health care improved in many parts of the country. The *New York Times* declared that in instituting these reforms, the shah had "aligned himself directly with workers and peasants and against conservatives and traditionalists."[5] Despite such praise, the shah's opponents remained steadfast, and none was more unyielding than Ayatollah Khomeini.

Unsurprisingly, the mullahs denounced the Shah's redistribution of their land and broader efforts to reduce their influence in his modern state. Back in 1942, a year after Reza Shah's abdication, Khomeini, then an unknown cleric, had written a book in which he described the ruler as a usurper who had ignored Islamic precepts and had overseen a cruel, corrupt, and illegitimate government. His subsequent declarations were filled with similar vitriol at the way in which the younger Pahlavi was substituting Western values for the Islamic tradition in Iran.

A collision between the cleric and the young monarch was inevitable. To the shah, "Islamism," or political Islam, was backward and antithetical to the country's needs. To Khomeini, the modernism that the shah espoused was tantamount to Westernism, and therefore tainted and abhorrent. Enfranchisement constituted an effort "to corrupt our chaste women." The Literacy Corps threatened the mullahs' monopoly as teachers, while land reform undermined their financial independence.

Reforms aside, the shah's government was wholly unacceptable to the ulama. In the eyes of Shiites, monarchs were inherently illegitimate unless they obtained the approval of the ayatollahs, who considered unlawful any regime that presumed to rule before the return of Islam's legendary Twelfth Imam. Moreover, the character of Iranian society under the Pahlavi dynasty—progressive, modern, secular, Western—ran directly counter to that envisioned and championed by conservative Muslim clerics. The importance of the imam, the head of a religious community, as a spiritual leader is at the heart of the Shiite doctrine. Imams lack the authority to change anything in the divine revelation of the Koran, but are authorized to interpret it through the divine guidance with which they are endowed. Shiites believe in the existence of 11 imams after Ali, the original successor of Muhammad. The Twelfth Imam is believed to have disappeared from human view around the ninth century, but still to exist in spirit. This "Hidden Imam" will one day reappear, and when he does, all the wrongs of the world will be righted, according to Shiite tradition.

In practical political terms, in the middle of the 20th century the Shiite ulama maintained that the shah—or anyone else who claimed governing authority before the return of the Hidden Imam—ruled unlawfully unless he was endorsed by the chief priests, the ayatollahs. The mullahs thus reserved the right to incite revolution to overthrow such rulers, and since the seventh century had done so. As a result, contemporary Iranians were accustomed to clerical denunciations of the shah's policies on the grounds that they were contrary to Islam. As the historian Barry Rubin observes in his seminal work, *Paved with Good Intentions*, "Tens of millions of Iranians, particularly those living in the rural villages and even the many peasants who had recently migrated to the cities, accepted these clerical proclamations as guides to proper behavior toward their king."[6]

Reza Shah had the mullahs' support when he pronounced himself king in 1926. At that time the mullahs were the country's principal teachers, and in many rural areas they had become prominent landowners who collected taxes on their property. But Reza Shah's introduction of reforms, including new civil, commercial, and penal codes that diminished the power of the ulama, coupled with his expansion of the secular school system, infuriated the entrenched clerics, whose power had shrunk considerably by the time he abdicated in 1941.

Ruhollah Khomeini's Islamism had deep roots. He was born in 1902, into a family that traced its ancestry to the Prophet Muhammad. His brothers became mullahs, and until the age of 60 Khomeini himself resided in the holy city of Qum, teaching law, philosophy, and ethics. He viewed Islam as an all-encompassing faith that prescribed a way of life with a commitment to the pursuit of social and political ideals. He had a gift for incendiary oratory, and his lectures attracted large crowds. The importance of Iranian independence and freedom from Eastern and Western colonialism was one of his constant themes.

As a Shiite, Khomeini may have been predisposed to dissent. Shiism differs radically from the Sunni faith practiced by most Muslims, mainly in its interpretations of the legacy of Muhammad and in the organized, hierarchical structure of its clergy. Shiism, as a minority branch in most of the Islamic world, has come to represent opposition to established power, which usually is held by the majority Sunnis. Shiism was imposed on Iran under the Safavid dynasty in the 16th century. For Iranians it has remained a source of political as well as religious identity.

Khomeini's views were stern. He seemed to believe in his view of the existence of good and of evil, with no gray area in between. He asserted that corruption cannot be reformed, so therefore must be destroyed. He frequently recounted a parable of a clean spring and a stagnant pond: the spring can pour into the pond, but the pond will remain stagnant unless it is drained.

His attack on the White Revolution was hardly the first time he had spoken out against Pahlavi policies. In the 1940s he published his view that the clergy must ensure that secular rule is limited by the laws of Islam. Later he declared, "From the beginning Islam represented a political power, not limiting itself to religious practice. In fact, if one refers to the practices of Muhammad, one sees that the texts about his life deal as much with politics, government, the struggle against tyrants, as with prayers."

In a 1941 text, "A Warning to the Nation," Khomeini sounded a theme that offered a rationale for a future Islamic Republic.

> When a government does not perform its duty, it becomes oppressive. If it does perform its duty, not only is it not oppressive, it is cherished and honored by God.
>
> The duty of government, therefore, must be clarified in order for us to establish whether the present government is oppressive or not.
>
> Reason and experience alike tell us that the governments now existing in the world were established at bayonet-point, by force. None of the monarchies or governments that we see in the world are based on justice or a correct foundation that is acceptable to reason. Their foundations are all rotten, being nothing but coercion and force. Reason can never accept that a man who is no different from others in

outward or inward accomplishments, unless maybe
he is inferior to them, should have his dictates considered proper and just and his government legitimate, merely because he has succeeded in gathering
around himself a gang to plunder the country and
murder its people. . . .

The only government that reason accepts as legitimate and welcomes freely and happily is the government of God, whose every act is just and whose
right it is to rule over the whole world and all the
particles of existence. Whatever He makes use of is
his own property, and whatever He takes, from
whomever He takes, is again his own property. No
men can deny this except the mentally disturbed.

It is in contrast with the government of God
that the nature of all existing governments becomes
clear, as well as the sole legitimacy of Islamic government. The duty of our government, which is
among the smaller states in the world, is to conform
to this legitimate government by making the laws
passed by the Majlis (religious council) a kind of
commentary on the divine law in the world, and that
its implementation will lead to the establishment of
the Virtuous City.

We do not say that government must be in the
hands of the faqih [priest]; rather we say that government must be run in accordance with God's law,
for the welfare of the country and the people demands this, and it is not feasible except with the su-
pervision of the religious leaders.[7]

When the land reform of the White Revolution began to take effect in 1963, the shah responded forcefully to those who resisted it. He derided the religious opposition as the "black reaction" (an allusion to their black robes) and dismissed the clerics as "lice-ridden mullahs." (At times he used the sneering epithet "ragheads.") Khomeini responded in kind, insisting that foreign enemies were the impetus for reform.

In June 1963 Khomeini denounced the shah as a Zionist agent and was arrested. His detention provoked widespread rioting, which the government brutally suppressed. Religious leaders convinced the shah not to execute Khomeini, and in the spring of 1964 he was released. The shah's emissaries tried to persuade the ayatollah to abandon politics, but Khomeini refused.

"All of Islam is politics," he replied.[8]

The breaking point between Khomeini and the shah involved relations with the United States. In July 1964 the government introduced a bill that made U.S. military advisers and their families accountable to American rather than Iranian courts. Such agreements on extraterritoriality are common where U.S. forces or advisers are stationed abroad, but in Iran the proposed legislation recalled humiliating capitulations demanded by the British and the Russians in the 19th and early 20th centuries.

Following the act's narrow passage by parliament, Khomeini denounced it as "a document for the enslavement of Iran." The Majlis, he said, had "acknowledged that Iran is a colony; it has given America a document attesting that the nation of Muslims is barbarous." In a vitriolic speech he attacked the subservient parliament and Iran's "ruling circles" for humiliating the country with the implication that "barbarous" local laws should not apply to foreigners. [9] His denunciation reinforced the perception of some Iranians that the shah was a puppet of the United States, while also illustrating Khomeini's skill at taking a relatively insignificant, albeit symbolic, issue like extraterritoriality—a kind of diplomatic immunity—and turning it into an incendiary cause célèbre.

Khomeini was rearrested and then expelled to Turkey in 1965. He soon moved to the Shia shrine in Najaf, Iraq, where he would remain until 1978. His bitterness toward the shah, whom he condemned as a "tyrant" and a "servant of the dollar," festered. In exile he continued to teach, write—his chief work was a 1970 volume, *Islamic Government*—and speak out against the shah. Tapes and transcripts of his speeches were smuggled into Iran and distributed widely through the mosques.

With Khomeini banished and the reforms progressing, the shah's fortunes were ascendant. In a 1966 book, *The White Revolution*, he expressed his interpretation of Iranian history and his role in it. On another front, he secured improved terms from foreign oil firms that effectively placed the National Iranian Oil Company in control of production. He amended the constitution in 1967 so that the queen would automatically become regent in the event of his death.

In 1971, at the ancient capital of Persepolis, the shah celebrated the 2,500th anniversary of Cyrus the Great's Persian Empire and the 30th anniversary of his own rule. He invited world leaders to the lavish, multimillion-dollar party, flying in food and wine from Maxim's in Paris and ordering uniforms by the couturier Lanvin for his attendant court, at a time when Iran's per capita income averaged $500 and a famine gripped the northern part of the country.

The shah's enemies were outraged by the opulent event and what it symbolized. On the same day as the state dinner at Persepolis, the Iranian consulate was bombed in San Francisco. A confederation of Iranian students at the University of California at Berkeley, claiming responsibility for the explosion, demonstrated near the consulate, shouting, "Death to the shah!"

More worrisome to his critics than the shah's inflated sense of self-importance was the economic divide in his country. While to outsiders Iran's economic progress seemed impressive, domestic opponents of the regime knew that the shah's reforms had mainly benefited the rich. An oil boom from 1963 until the late 1970s had been accompanied by an increase in per capita GNP, from about $200 to $1,000 in real terms—one of the steepest rises in recent history for a sizable country. But critics contended that the gains were concentrated in the upper income levels, largely as a result of government policies. The shah's grand anniversary party came to be viewed as a vivid illustration of the ever-widening gulf between the rulers and the ruled.

Khomeini denounced the Persepolis celebration from Najaf. "Anyone who organizes or participates in these festivals is a traitor to Islam and the Iranian nation," he declared. The shah's designation as King of Kings, said Khomeini, "is the most hated of all titles in the sight of God. . . . Islam is fundamentally opposed to the whole notion of monarchy. . . . Monarchy is one of the most shameful and disgraceful reactionary manifestations."[10]

At the OPEC meetings in late 1973, the shah pushed successfully for a redoubling of prices, arguing with some justification that oil prices had been kept low while the prices of other commodities had risen. The shah predicted that Iran would soon become one of the world's five great powers, with an average income equal to the best of them. He did not seem to realize, however, that huge revenues could not simply be infused into the Iranian economy without courting the risks of inflation and shortages.

It wasn't modernization that was undermining the shah, but the growing disparity between Iran's haves and have-nots. Increasingly, his opponents decried the societal inequities that existed at a time when oil revenues approached $20 billion a year after the price rise. Moreover, there was little freedom of speech or of the press, and opposition was routinely and often ruthlessly suppressed, particularly after the emergence of guerilla groups in the 1960s and '70s.

Beginning in 1976, large-scale demonstrations, usually demanding greater adherence to fundamentalist Islamic practices, took place with greater frequency. But instead of meeting the challenge directly, the shah alternated between harsh repressive measures and attempts at appeasement (for example, his return to the use of the Arab calendar in the fall of 1978). In the second half of the 1970s the shah found himself increasingly beset by his Islamic opponents.

One historian observed, "The clergy was the only group in Iran equipped to engage in oppositional activities. It possessed a functioning system of communications; local facilities in the form of mosques and related buildings . . . close daily contact with the masses and the possibility of including political themes in the Friday sermons. With all this, the high-ranking clergy enjoyed a certain degree of immunity from the shah's grip."[11]

With his election in 1976, Jimmy Carter became the eighth U.S. president to serve during the shah's reign, which had begun 35 years earlier. For the shah—and for the future relationship between the two countries—he was also the worst. At times indecisive, at times uninformed; at times a friend to the shah, at other times his critic, Carter was forever behind the curve when it came to Iran, always reacting to—but never anticipating—rapidly changing events. In the final analysis he proved unable to support and preserve a longtime ally's government and his own nation's vital strategic relationship with Iran.

From the outset, the Carter administration failed to grasp the reality and significance of events unfolding inside Iran. In particular, the administration failed to appreciate that Islamism, or political Islam, was the force behind a steadily intensifying rebellion against the shah's rule. Moreover, a number of administration officials were frankly unsympathetic to the shah and disinclined to support him.

Writes analyst Mohsen M. Milani, "With the new administration came a breed of ideologues and bureaucrats who sincerely wished to weaken, and if possible to sever, U.S. ties with the despotic regimes of the Third World. Products of the antiwar and civil rights movements, they orchestrated a selective campaign against some countries that were in violation of human rights. Iran and Nicaragua were the favorite targets."

Zbigniew Brzezinski, Carter's national security adviser, confirms this portrayal, asserting that "The lower echelons at [the] State [Department], notably the head of [the] Iran desk, Henry Precht, were motivated by [a] doctrinal dislike of the shah and simply wanted him out of power altogether." Brzezinski described an administration that was simultaneously pulled in opposite directions, with disastrous results: "Once Carter was inaugurated, his sincere moralistic concerns had to be balanced against the U.S. strategic and economic interests in Iran. Gradually, therefore, the humanitarian rhetoric of the administration and its actual foreign policy became worlds apart, almost hypocritical." [12] Moral absolutism, contrary to geopolitical pragmatism, defines Carter.

The shah found Carter difficult to read. From the time of his first White House visit, in November 1977, the Iranian monarch considered his relationship with this White House to be uneasy. The new administration had emphasized that he was still regarded as an important ally, but unrestricted arms sales to Iran could not continue if the repressive practices of SAVAK, the shah's secret police force, persisted.

In fact, the shah had initiated significant changes even before Carter's inauguration. To curry favor with Washington, he had begun his ambitious program of liberalization in early 1977. The reforms included free elections, reduced censorship of the press, and judicial procedures that ended torture by SAVAK and substantially enhanced the rights of political prisoners. Economic and educational measures were also enacted. The reforms had the undesired effect of emboldening the shah's opponents, however, and thus paving the way for the nascent revolutionary movement. Milani writes,

> But the most profound impact of Carter's human rights policy and the shah's liberalization initiatives was psychological: They changed the attitude

of the opposition to the shah and the shah himself. The U.S. human rights policy generated a perception in Iran that Washington's previous policy of unconditional support for the shah had changed and that Carter was pressuring the shah to reform his political system. Gradually, this perception gained more and more acceptance among Iranians. Whether or not this perception was accurate, it gave the opposition a new lease on life, strengthened the spirit of defiance among the population, and slowly shattered the myth of the shah's invincibility, a myth SAVAK had so painstakingly created in Iran. [13]

In this newly liberalized climate the shah rocked back on his heels. He would refrain from brutal retaliation against his opponents, who consequently exhibited a newfound boldness. In September 1977 Khomeini wrote to the ulama: "Today in Iran, a break is in sight; take advantage of this opportunity. . . . Today, the writers of political parties criticize; they voice their opposition; and they write letters to the shah and to the ruling class and sign those letters. You, too, should write, and a few of the Maraja' should sign it. Write about the difficulties and declare to the world the crimes of the shah. Write the criticism and submit it to them [the authorities], as a few other people who have done so and have said many other things and nobody has bothered them."[14]

The shah was proud that *Time* magazine had noted his commitment to a program of liberalization, and that his prime minister had moved to end press censorship and even freed several hundred political prisoners. The shah recalled the appraisal that appeared in *Time*: "In a few months, the police-state atmosphere has altered drastically to a mood of vastly greater individual freedom and relaxation."[15]

In addition, the shah optimistically surmised, my talks with President Carter had gone well. Iran's relationship with the U.S. had been so deep and so friendly during the last three administrations—I had counted Lyndon Johnson, Richard Nixon and Gerald Ford among my friends—that it seemed only natural that our friendship would continue. After all, good relations were in the best interests of both nations. Carter appeared to be a smart man. [16]

Carter and the shah met for a second and final time a few weeks later in 1977. It was New Year's Eve in Tehran, and the two leaders exchanged toasts. The shah spoke first:

> In our country, according to ancient tradition, the visit of the first guest in the new year is an omen for that year. And although the annual new year is celebrated with the advent of spring, nevertheless, since the distinguished guest tonight is such a person of good will and achievement, naturally we consider it as a most excellent omen. [17]

The shah further elaborated on the "distinctive qualities of the great American nation" that had always been "highly regarded by us," among them humanitarianism and liberty. He further thanked the United States for its "unforgettable" role during the past Iranian crises, no doubt alluding to his CIA-assisted return to power after the Mossadeq crisis in 1953.

The high point of the evening was Jimmy Carter's toast. Administration aide Pierre Salinger was startled by the contrast between Carter's typically "unexceptional" speaking style and the "startling" message he delivered. The president eloquently evoked his concern for human rights in Iran by quoting Saadi, one of Iran's best-loved poets:

> Human beings are like parts of a body,
> Created from the same essence,
> When one part is hurt and in pain, others
> Cannot remain in peace and be quiet
> If the misery of others leaves you indifferent
> And with no feelings of sorrow, then you
> Cannot be called a human being.

The shah's opposition would surely have found encouragement in these sensitive words, which seemed to support the struggle against the monarchy.

But Carter then turned 180 degrees, lavishing on the shah fulsome praise that would come back to haunt him, as riots soon unfolded across Iran. Within 12 months the spreading unrest would culminate in the fall of the long-reigning shah. The president continued,

> Iran, because of the great leadership of the shah, is an island of stability in one of the more troubled areas of the world. This is a great tribute to you, Your Majesty, and to your leadership and to the respect and admiration and the love which your people give to you. . . .
>
> As I drove through the streets of Tehran today with the shah, we saw literally thousands of Iranian citizens standing beside the street with a friendly at-

titude, expressing their welcome to me. And I also saw hundreds, perhaps even thousands of American citizens who stood there welcoming their president in a nation which has taken them to heart and made them feel at home. . . .

The cause of human rights is one that also is shared deeply by our people and by the leaders of our two nations. . . .

We have no other nation on earth who is closer to us in planning for our mutual military security. We have no other nation with whom we have closer consultation on regional problems that concern us both. And there is no leader with whom I have a deeper sense of personal gratitude and personal friendship. [18]

The president's sentiments continued in this expansive vein. "Our talks have been priceless," he said. "Our friendship is irreplaceable, and my own gratitude is to the shah, who in his wisdom and with his experience has been so helpful to me, a new leader." The shah leapt to his feet, grasping the president's right hand in both of his and shaking it vigorously. "He was beaming," Salinger recalled. "No American president had ever hailed him so warmly."[19]

American officials at the banquet were understandably dumbfounded by this glowing testament. After all, much of Carter's campaign platform a year earlier was founded on human rights. Wrote Salinger,

From the day the President had enumerated his human rights policy, I had felt that the time would come when it would conflict with the national interest. It had been my experience that whenever such a conflict occurs, it is the special policy that gives way, no matter how sincerely it was initiated. That phenomenon was never more evident than on the night of December 31, 1977, when Carter's human rights policy was confronted by the need of the United States to maintain a strong ally in the Middle East. That ally was Iran. [20]

But alas, in practical terms that human rights policy never did give way. Little if anything in the crucial ensuing year of 1978 would validate Carter's expression of gratitude and friendship. The shah's twin sister, Princess Ashraf, later wrote that as Carter spoke, "I looked at his pale face. I thought his smile was artificial, his eyes icy—and I hoped I could trust him."[21] In the months that followed she would decide that she could not. Carter's confused message aided the insurgents.

Although the Carter administration did not put any serious human rights pressure on the shah, the support of the administration for human rights generally made it easy for the Iranian opposition, with its exaggerated belief in American influence over the shah, to conclude that the shah had been given his human rights marching orders. When the monarchy cracked down, the opposition forces, in line with their obsession with foreign influence, drew the reverse conclusion—the United States had now ordered the shah to reestablish a policy of repression.

Carter's contradictory stance on human rights did not escape the notice of the opposition religious leaders in Iran. After the shah received from Carter the $10 billion worth of military goods he wanted during the latter's New

Year's visit in 1977, the opposition concluded that Carter was a dangerous hypocrite. It was on February 19, 1978, the beginning of a tumultuous year of almost monthly protests and violent riots in Iran, that Khomeini spoke out on Carter's policy of human rights.

> Carter says human rights are inalienable, and then he says, "I don't want to hear about human rights." Of course, he's right from his own point of view; he uses the logic of bandits. The head of a government that has signed the Declaration of Human Rights says, "We have military bases in Iran; we can't talk about human rights there. Respect for human rights is feasible only in countries where we have no military bases." [22]

Despite Carter's effusive praise for the shah, it was his administration's prevailing view—that the shah was an authoritarian leader who must curb his regime's excesses—that shaped the administration's treatment of him from 1977 until his flight into exile, in January 1979. One analyst noted, "The people of Iran quietly watched the exchange of visits between President Carter and the shah. When new policies finally emerged, the violence began."[23]

Iran's strategic importance was indisputable. At this time 30 percent of U.S. oil imports came from the Persian Gulf. (The Gulf also supplied 60 percent of Western Europe's imported oil and 70 percent of Japan's). For the United States and its allies, an independent Iran had long meant a guaranteed oil supply and a linchpin for the maintenance of Western interests in the Middle East.

Iran, in turn, was an important export market for the

United States, purchasing well over $2 billion worth of American goods each year and thus ranking in the top ten of this nation's overseas customers. In the next decade, the 1980s, the sale of nuclear technology to Iran was expected to increase the total value of U.S. exports to the shah's country by approximately $12 billion. No prudent U.S. administration could afford to overlook this aspect of Iran's importance.

Carter's glowing remarks that New Year's Eve may well have been partly intended to assuage any uncertainty the shah felt about Democratic U.S. presidents. It was during the Republican administration of Dwight D. Eisenhower that the shah had been returned to power after he was deposed in 1953. A military buildup of Iran accelerated during the Republican Nixon administration and continued thereafter, with some $20 billion in U.S.-made weaponry sold to Iran between 1973 and 1978—about 17 times the amount sent to Iran in the previous 20 years.

Thus, given Iran's evident strategic importance to the United States, the Carter administration should have been fully aware of the gravity of the crisis facing the shah by late 1977. As early as July 25 of that year, the U.S. embassy in Tehran had sent an airgram to Washington entitled "Straws in the Wind: Intellectual and Religious Opposition in Iran," which described the nature of the shah's opponents. Seven months later a similar, more detailed study arrived.

The shah's regime was in steady decline throughout 1978. As I stated in the Introduction, a major precipitating event was the January 1978 publication of the newspaper article defaming Ayatollah Khomeini as some kind of medieval reactionary. The article ignited widespread protests and riots, which included frequent calls for revolution. The killing of a number of protestors failed to dent the opposition's resolve. Some demonstrations attracted crowds of over 100,000, signaling the magnitude of the unrest among the populace. On January 9, 1978, nearly 4,000 religious students in Qum demanded, among other things, that the absolute monarchy surrender power to a constitutional government. The march ended in bloodshed when troops killed dozens and wounded hundreds of others.

A blueprint for the type of government that the rioters demanded could be found in the Iranian constitution of 1906–11. This document, which held a special meaning for Iranians, had become a rallying point for the opposition to the shah. The constitution declared that sovereignty rests with the people; that the government's executive, legislative, and judicial powers should be separate; and that individual rights must be protected. According to Article 39 of the 1907 fundamental laws, the shah is required in his oath as king "to be the guardian of the constitutional law of Iran, to reign in conformity with the established laws, and to promote and protect Twelver Imam Shi'ism."

Mohammed Reza Shah, however, had ruled more as an essentially absolute monarch, controlling all of the government's important powers and functions.[23]

Despite receiving ample intelligence on the growing turmoil in Iran, Washington failed to act in support of its staunchest ally in the region. Indeed, the administration consistently appeared to misread the political pulse of Iran. "Available documents about United States policy in this phase are contradictory and reflect the self-delusion of the policymakers," Milani writes. "The U.S. foreign policy establishment, having for so long supported the shah, was sluggish in adjusting to Iran's revolutionary situation. In one corner, the CIA in late August 1978 concluded that 'Iran was not in a revolutionary or even pre-revolutionary situation' and across the way the Defense Intelligence Agency (DIA) predicted in September that 'the shah is expected to remain actively in power for the next ten years.'[24]

By late summer in 1978, the situation was dire. After months of violent demonstrations and riots, including an August 19 arson fire at a cinema in Abadan in which more than 400 people burned to death—despite inconclusive evidence, their deaths were widely blamed on SAVAK—the shah's rule was obviously imperiled. His opposition was divided into two factions: the moderates, including the National Front, the Liberation Movement, and orthodox ulama led by Ayatollah Shariatmadari, who advocated peaceful reform; and the revolutionary camp, including guerilla groups in addition to Ayatollah Khomeini's adherents, which favored radical change.

The shah's August 1978 appointment of Ja'far Sharif Imami, a former prime minister, to reconcile the warring factions and preserve his monarchy by appeasing the fundamentalists through a wide-ranging program of concessions, failed. Through the appointment and other measures the shah had hoped to placate the Shiite establishment and the rioting masses by opening channels of communication with the religious leaders and replacing key ministers and government officials with individuals more palatable to the clerics.[25]

Nevertheless, religious opposition to the shah continued unabated, reaching a boiling point on September 8, when more than 100,000 citizens assembled in Tehran's Jaleh Square, ostensibly to pray and observe the end of Ramadan. While prayer might have been the original intent of the gathering, a far different agenda played out. Over a period of 72 hours the tone of the speeches grew increasingly strident, as pro-Khomeini demonstrators denounced the monarchy and called for the establishment of an Islamic government. Fearing that the demonstrators would overrun its troops, the government declared martial law in 12 major cities at six o'clock on the morning of September 8, but neglected to inform the demonstrators of the edict.

Accounts of what happened differ. It is clear that the troops fired, at first over the heads of demonstrators. Then they fired at them. Some witnesses claim there was provocation; that men standing behind women and children fired at the soldiers. Others claim that when the soldiers ordered them to disperse, the protestors threw brickbats, prompting the troops to open fire on their antagonists. One account said that a soldier shot his commanding officer and then himself rather than obey an order to massacre demonstrators. The mob rampaged afterward, stoning banks and post offices, igniting bonfires and creating barricades in streets to slow the movement of tanks, which roamed the town, firing at people. The momentous, bloody clash would be known thereafter as Black Friday. [26]

According to the government, 86 protesters had been slain. The opposition maintained, implausibly, that 3,000 had died. The shah, already suffering from the cancer that would prove fatal, was devastated by the event. He offered further concessions to his opponents, but it was too late; by this time his long-ruling government was almost certainly doomed. An ensuing government crackdown included a reimposition of censorship and the detention of several opposition leaders. A well-publicized call from

President Carter followed the mayhem. He pledged his support for the shah.

But the shah had decided a year earlier that repression of the opposition could not salvage his regime. "I can repress. I can control as long as I'm alive," he said. "But when I'm gone the situation will blow up in the face of my son." Accordingly, he attempted to reach an accommodation with his opponents through measures such as relaxing restrictions on the press and releasing some 1,500 political prisoners. But the latter move backfired: Families whose imprisoned relatives were not among those released leapt to the conclusion that they had been killed. Meanwhile, many released prisoners publicly recounted the years of torture they had suffered, further inflaming anti-shah passions.

In the summer of 1978 William Sullivan, the U.S. ambassador to Iran, was aware of the depth and intensity of the shah's opposition. Inexplicably, however, it took Sullivan until January 1979 to surmise that if the shah's army were to confront Khomeini's revolutionary cadres, the revolutionaries were likely to prevail.

Sullivan's own accounts of events are revealing. On November 9, 1978, he sent his "Thinking the Unthinkable" communiqué to Washington. In it he noted that "conventional wisdom" held that stability in Iran rested on two pillars: the monarchy and the Shiite religion. While for the past 15 years the "religious pillar had been largely subordinate to the monarchic," that relationship had now changed.

The ambassador urged Washington to prepare for a contingency whereby the shah and much of his military would leave the country; in order to prepare, the United

States should support a rapprochement between Khomeini and a moderate government. Sullivan recalled that his cable caused "consternation" in Washington: "It was the first time he (Carter) became aware that the shah might not survive. If this [was] so, it must either be [because] he was so preoccupied with the Camp David process that he had neglected to notice our cables, or else that his national security briefers had chosen not to trouble him with the problems in Iran."[27]

Carter later wrote in *Time* magazine, "The shah was trying to decide whether to set up an interim government, set up a military government or even abdicate. We encouraged him to hang firm and count on our backing.

"However, it was becoming increasingly evident that the shah was no longer functioning as a strong leader, but was growing despondent and unsure of himself. . . . I sent him a message stating that whatever action he took, including setting up a military government, I would support him ... There was no question in my mind that the shah deserved our unequivocal support."[28]

But it was too little, too late. Despite these recollections about "unequivocal support," Sullivan's bemused recollections of the events were most telling.

Whatever the situation in Washington, and whatever the motivations of the individuals involved, I did not seem able to get any serious [response to] "thinking the unthinkable" by those responsible for policy formulation. My normal experience with cables of this sort led me to expect that a significant review of our policy would take place in Washington and that I would receive some guidance concerning

the attitudes of our administration toward my rec-
ommendations. I waited in vain for any such response.
In fact, the cable was never answered by Washington.

We drifted through the remainder of November
and into December with no guidance from the Department of State or from Washington in general.
The Department of State spokesman and the president himself publicly reasserted the administration's
support of the shah. These pronouncements were
made with such regularity that they became something of a joke among the American news media.[29]

Meanwhile, the shah was receiving conflicting advice
from various parties. Sullivan and Ambassador Anthony
Parsons of Britain warned him that a repressive crackdown on the opposition would be unacceptable and urged
him to resolve the crisis peacefully. In contrast, Brzezinski
and other hardliners advocated a tough stance, exhorting
the shah to rescind his reforms and arrest opposition leaders. Ultimately, the shah opted to seek a peaceful resolution
of the crisis, although he refused to relinquish power.

Appearing on television, the shah sought to project an
air of humility, referring to himself as *padishah* ("king") instead of the title he always demanded, *shahanshah*, ("king of
kings"). He promised before a national audience to make
amends for his past errors and transgressions. He permitted the arrest of 132 government leaders, including the
former prime minister, Amir Abbas Hoveyda, and former
SAVAK chief, General Ne'matollah Nasiri.

A month later, however, the shah exacerbated his
problems by requesting that Iraq expel Khomeini from
Najaf. Denied entry to Kuwait, the ayatollah sought asylum

in France. French President Giscard d'Estaing solicited the view of the shah, who imprudently approved Khomeini's relocation. The shah's assumption that the dissident cleric would be less of a threat in distant, Christian France than in a neighboring Islamic country proved wrong. He had neglected to consider the power of modern communications. Using long-distance telephone connections from Paris to Tehran, Khomeini received daily reports on the growing unrest in Iran. Moreover, Khomeini read his sermons directly into Iranian tape recorders for instant distribution on cassettes through the mullah network across the country. In this way he was able to organize meetings and demonstrations involving the clergy and his followers.

In addition, the world's media now had unfettered access to the ayatollah. His pronouncements were published and broadcast almost daily. By the end of 1978 the ayatollah had cultivated an image as a saintly old man who was determined to establish in Iran a more just, democratic, and "spiritual" government than the despotic Shah's re-gime. While the name Ruhollah Khomeini means "inspired of God," Milton Viorst, author of *The Shadow of the Prophet*, maintains that "Khomeini is best understood within the context of the deep feelings of nationalism, rather than of piety, that swept through Iran during his long lifetime." Indeed, as his thinking evolved, Khomeini found reason to examine anew his earlier conviction that a rededication to the Islamic faith was enough by itself to save Muslim society.

His lectures in the 1970s developed his theory of *velayat-e faqih*, conventionally translated as "the mandate of the jurist" and denoting a concept of government by jurisconsult, i.e., experts in Islamic law. "The mandate of the jurist," Khomeini said, "is to govern and administer the country and implement the provisions of the sacred law. Since Islamic government is a government of law, those acquainted with the law or, more precisely, with religion must supervise its functioning. It is they who supervise all executive and administrative affairs."[30]

The ayatollah was not speaking theoretically. He was preparing the ground for his own future leadership of the Islamic Republic of Iran. He suggested the presence of a divine right in the jurist's role when he said, "The jurist's regency will be the same as enjoyed by the Prophet in governing the Islamic community and it is incumbent on all Muslims to obey him."

Meanwhile, internal divisions within the Carter administration undermined its foreign policy. Cyrus Vance, the secretary of state, argued that the United States could not in good conscience ask the leader of another country to order a military crackdown on his own people. But Brzezinski, the tough-minded, pragmatic national security adviser, was privately advising the shah to do just that: deploy his army to crush the rebellion that was being orchestrated from afar by Khomeini. Brzezinski believed that the character of the shah's regime was secondary to its strategic importance to U.S. interests in the Middle East, and that the shah should therefore be encouraged to secure control of his country by any means necessary. In contrast, Vance "was eager to demonstrate that the old Kissingerian geopolitical view of the world had been abandoned in favor of a more moralistic approach," writes Michael Ledeen.[31]

The president, meanwhile, bestrode a nebulous middle ground between the opposing camps. Carter, says Milani, "preoccupied with the negotiations for SALT II and the Camp David Accord, paid little attention to Iran during the early phases of the revolutionary movement. When he did focus on Iran, his record was one of oscillation between the two factions."[32] The shah was understandably confused by the administration's mixed message, observes Ledeen:

> Throughout the crisis, the shah was convinced that the American government had a grand strategy for Iran, even though its outlines remained obscure to him. He was certain of the existence of an American strategy, for the geopolitical stakes in the Iranian crisis were so great that it was inconceivable to him that the United States had not developed such a plan. His own life demonstrated the consistency of American activity in his country. He had been restored to the throne in 1953 thanks to the Americans and their British allies. Throughout the 1960s he had to cope with American efforts to force a particular political direction upon his country; the might of the Iranian military, for all its defaults a determinant force in the region, stemmed directly from the United States; the new industries and the new cities were inhabited by tens of thousands of American technicians and their families; and the special relationship in the early 1970s combined with fortuitous increases in oil prices had made Iran one of the United States' most important allies.
>
> The shah believed that this continued American interest in Iran had not been the result of personal sympathy for himself or admiration for his methods. American support was based rather on a cold-blooded analysis of American interest. And he

reasoned, what had taken place to change his position? Was the United States not compelled to ensure
the existence of a reliable Iran? Had he not been a
good ally? What could the Americans hope to gain if
he were overthrown?[33]

As the Camp David meetings on the Middle East continued, the unrest in Iran threatened to boil over. The shah
recalled,

> I have been told that some Americans, Israelis,
> and Egyptians taking part in those meetings ex-
> pressed considerable concern about the events in
> my country. Some reports suggested that Israeli
> spokesmen told the Americans that Iran was more
> important than their own negotiations. If so, I had
> no knowledge of it, nor did these warnings have
> much effect on American action. . . . But I do know
> that reports widely circulated in the West about a
> Carter telephone call to me are false. President Car-
> ter has never called me—except once at Lackland
> Air Force Base in December 1979. . . . For the next
> four months the only word I ever received from Mr.
> Sullivan was a reiteration of Washington's complete
> support for my rule. To be more specific, the U.S.
> backed me 100 percent and hoped I would establish
> law and order, as well as continue my program of
> political liberalization.
>
> For the balance of the year I received numerous
> messages from various people in and out of the
> Carter Administration pledging U.S. support. When-
> ever I met Sullivan and asked him to confirm these

official statements, he promised he would.

But a day or two later he would return, gravely shake his head and say that he had received "no in-structions" and therefore could not comment. . . . He seemed to take seriously everything I said to him. But his answer was always the same: I received no instructions. Is it any wonder that I felt increasingly isolated and cut off from my Western friends? What were they really thinking, what did they want—for Iran and of me? I was never told. I never knew.

Sullivan, and the British ambassador, Anthony Parsons, who so often accompanied him, met in a stiff diplomatic ballet that ended without resolution of any kind. Meanwhile, I was forced to deal with what is usually described as a pre-revolutionary situa-tion. In truth, it was the end of modern civilization in Iran. . . . Since then I have often been asked why I did not seek the confirmation I wanted through other channels, perhaps by picking up the telephone and calling Washington. My answer is simple. In for-eign affairs, I have always observed the protocol of international diplomacy. Thus, I never tried to estab-lish direct contact with Carter or anyone else in the Administration because that is done through an am-bassador. The fact that no one contacted me during the crisis in any official way explains everything about the American attitude. I did not know it then—perhaps I did not want to know—but it is clear to me now that the Americans wanted me out.[34]

When student riots broke out at the University of Tehran in November 1978, government soldiers opened fire on the demonstrators. The shah, disinclined to reach Carter directly, arranged to talk with Brzezinski, who called Tehran on November 3 though the switchboard of the Iranian embassy in Washington. Brzezinski encouraged the shah to take whatever measures he deemed necessary, with the full assurance that Washington would "back him to the hilt." Brzezinksi later told friends that the shah should never have had any doubts about American support, even if the monarch decided to form a military government. But U.S. actions—and inaction—often suggested otherwise.

Both Brzezinski and Defense Secretary James Schlesinger worried that a collapse of the shah's regime might have catastrophic international effects above and beyond the outcome in Iran itself. Although they differed slightly on the proper American response to the crisis, they agreed on Iran's geopolitical importance to the United States. Both recognized that a hostile or even neutral Iran would seriously compromise American influence in and around the Persian Gulf.

On November 19, 1978, Soviet Premier Leonid Brezhnev issued a warning to Carter about the consequences of any U.S. intervention to save the shah:

> It must be clear that any interference, especially military interference in the affairs of Iran—a State which directly borders on the Soviet Union—would be regarded as a matter affecting security interests. . . The events taking place in that country constitute purely internal affairs, and the questions involved in them should be decided by the Iranians—the Shah has ruled with an iron will.[35]

With a line thus drawn in the sand, Carter had yet another chance to demonstrate his country's commitment to Iran. Instead, Secretary Vance responded with a feeble declaration the following day: "The United States will continue to support the shah in his efforts to restore domestic tranquillity. . . . [T]he United States does not intend to interfere in the affairs of another country."[36]

Foreign observers were entitled to conclude that the United States had deserted the shah.

This impression was strengthened on December 7 when a reporter at a press conference asked Carter if the shah was expected to prevail. "I don't know. I hope so. This is something in the hands of the people of Iran," came the president's lukewarm response. He continued: "We have never had any intention and don't have any intention of trying to intercede in the internal political affairs of Iran. We primarily want an absence of bloodshed, and stability. We personally prefer that the shah maintain a major role in the government, but that's a decision for the Iranian people to make."[37]

The finality of the message was unmistakable. In the words of one analyst, "Everyone who mattered in Iran knew the Americans were dumping the shah."

In mid-December 1978, Richard Helms, the former United States ambassador to Iran (1973–76), weighed in, saying he found "Washington's response [to developments in Iran] lethargic and uncomprehending."[38]

Events transpiring in Iran were confusing. In a meeting with Iranian Prime Minister Azhari on December 20, Sullivan deduced that the monarchy could not survive, as the shah remained incapable of implementing a decisive course of action. The overriding need to restore law and order had become a Sisyphean task. The shah had instructed Azrahi to order the government's troops to administer martial law by shooting into the air, over the heads of rioters and protestors. The troops had been deployed in the streets for nearly four months, however, and were utterly demoralized by the orders, which prohibited them from responding effectively to abuse from demonstrators. At a pivotal point in their meeting Azrahi leaned toward Sullivan and said, gravely, "You must understand this and you must tell it to your government. This country is lost because the king cannot make up his mind."[39]

Sullivan reported to Washington that, as he had predicted in his November cable, the military had failed to restore law and order and the downfall of the shah was inevitable. Consequently, Sullivan proposed to meet with the opposition and the military, in hopes of forging an agreement that would prevent the annihilation of the weakened armed forces. Two days later he received a reply from Washington, in which the administration feebly and pointlessly insisted that the United States "continued to support the Shah" and expected his government to survive the current crisis.[40]

As the year drew to a close, the president announced that former Deputy Secretary of State George Ball had been enlisted as a consultant to the government on the issue of Iran. While Ball was sympathetic to the shah's efforts to survive, he suspected that the monarchy was doomed. Accordingly, Ball proposed the creation of a transition plan that would enable moderate Iranian political elements to succeed the shah and, it was hoped, prevent a revolution. Alas, the Ball analysis went for naught, as the White House rejected his recommendation. No copy of the report ever reached the United States embassy in Tehran.

Sullivan and his aides took it upon themselves to meet in Teheran with leaders of the domestic "liberation movement" opposed to the shah. Those leaders advised the ambassador that over a hundred current senior military officers would be expected to resign their positions and leave the country when the shah departed. Their vacated positions would be filled by qualified members of their movement. In addition, they assured Sullivan that no arrests or other acts of revenge would occur in the wake of the shah's abdication and that the core of the armed forces could be kept intact.

Sullivan found these views encouraging, but he wanted to ensure that they were acceptable to Ayatollah Khomeini and his group in Paris. The American diplomat feared that the ayatollah, having made a triumphant return to Iran, would employ his powerful rhetoric to subvert the liberation movement's proposal to preserve the military.

Sullivan thus recommended that the U.S. government send a senior emissary to Paris to begin discussions with the ayatollah. He prepared talking points indicating that the United States' primary concern was to maintain Iran's territorial integrity and keep its armed forces generally intact. He added that any conflict between the Islamic revolutionary forces and the Iranian military would benefit only the Soviet Union and its agents inside Iran.

Secretary of State Vance chose Theodore L. Eliot, the inspector general of the foreign services, who had just returned from four years as U.S. ambassador to Afghanistan, to serve as the senior emissary. "He had a quick mind and a direct demeanor and was an excellent choice for the mission," Sullivan recalled. "I felt comforted that he would be able to deal on positive terms with the ayatollah."[41]

The shah had asked to be kept informed. Sullivan was told that Eliot would leave for Paris on January 6. Sullivan noted that Vance had just returned to Washington after traveling for most of November and December on matters related to the Camp David peace process. Wrote Sullivan, "Thus he had been out of touch with Iran, so there was a new precision in my dealings with Washington. At the Guadeloupe summit meeting that had just ended, President Carter had met with French President Giscard d'Estaing, German Chancellor Helmut Schmidt, and Japanese Prime Minister Ohira. All had convinced Carter that the shah was doomed and that it was extremely prudent to accept some accommodations in order to protect our national interests in this vital part of the world. The Eliot mission could go a long way toward achieving that objective."

But the mission would be inexplicably canceled by Washington before it had a chance to succeed. Said Sullivan, "My surprise and anguish could not have been more complete. . . . The shah was to be advised that we no longer intended to have any discussions with Ayatollah Khomeini."

Sullivan recalled what followed:

> I sent a short message to Secretary Vance saying that I thought the president had made a gross mistake and that a cancellation for the Eliot mission would be an irretrievable error. I urged that the decision be rescinded and the mission be restored . . .
>
> I received a terse reply. It informed me that not only the president but the vice president, the secretary of state, the secretary of defense, the secretary of the treasury, the head of the CIA, and the national

security adviser had all agreed with the president on
his decision to cancel the mission. I was therefore instructed to proceed as previously directed. 42

Despite the unanimity within the administration on
the mission's cancellation, Sullivan knew that "the United
States was facing the situation in Iran with no policy whatsoever." The shah's demise was, in his estimation, "inevitable." The ambassador proved correct on both counts:
the only U.S. policy on Iran was the absence of a policy. An
explosive end to the Pahlavi dynasty was imminent.

Sullivan then had to deliver the bad news to the shah.
When asked why the mission had been canceled, Sullivan
could offer no explanation. An agitated shah asked "how
we expected to influence these people if we would not
even talk with them. He threw up his hands in despair and
asked what we intended to do now. I had no answer," Sullivan recalls.

Until the cancellation of the Eliot mission, the shah
had believed that the United States harbored "some grand
national design that was intended to save his country," said
Sullivan, adding that it finally became painfully clear to the
Iranian ruler that "we had no design whatsoever and that
our government's actions were being guided by some inexplicable whim."43

On January 12 Sullivan made yet another effort to
persuade Washington to act forcefully. "I sent off a cable
saying that 'our national interests demand that we attempt
to structure a *modus vivendi* between the military and the religious [factions], in order to preempt the Tudeh,'" he recalls. The cable also warned of disastrous consequences
should the United States be perceived as supporting the

shah at this late stage. Sullivan's impassioned missive was addressed directly to President Carter, but his pleas were unavailing: "As usual, I received no answer to this cable and no indication that the White House comprehended the nature of the situation developing in Iran," he recalls.[44]

In retrospect, the U.S. government was always at least one long step behind the realities of the Iranian revolution. The Carter administration failed to obtain adequate intelligence about internal factors in Iran; to heed the reports it received from Sullivan and other informed observers; to comprehend the threat posed by Khomeini and his radical followers; and to consider using force when the shah's precarious position was finally undeniable.

Where does the fault lie? The buck stops at the top. After the Bay of Pigs fiasco in 1961, President Kennedy remarked that success has many fathers, but failure is an orphan. Just as Kennedy accepted responsibility for that abject failure, Jimmy Carter should be held accountable for his administration's grievous mistakes and their far-reaching consequences.

Throughout the growing crisis, the Carter administration functioned in a strange twilight zone, an impenetrable fog, nearly paralyzed by misinformation and internecine feuding. The words of CIA director Admiral Stansfield Turner suggest the administration's ineptitude, albeit in mild terms: "If we had been more sensitive to the cumulative effect of the rate of change in Iran, American policy might have been different," he said. Two months later Turner backpedaled, however, telling an interviewer, "Even if I'd told the policymakers on October 5 that there was going to be a major upheaval on November 5 in Iran, there was nothing they could do."

Brzezinski, for one, found the performance of Turner and his agency shockingly maladroit and unhelpful. Recalling a high-level policy meeting on November 6, 1978, he writes, "There was also a futile discussion of the Iranian opposition, with Admiral Turner indicating that, because of prior restrictions on contact with the opposition (restrictions also applied by Sullivan) he did not have much information to share with us." The national security adviser added: "I was really appalled by how inept and vague Stan Turner's comments on the crisis in Iran were. This reinforces my strong view that we need much better political intelligence."[45]

According to analyst Burton I. Kaufman, such intelligence was so fragmentary that only as late as November 1978—when it was nearly too late to stem Iran's revolutionary tide—did the Carter administration grasp the magnitude of Khomeini's popular support. "Even then," says Kaufman, "officials were as worried about leftist infiltration of the militants as about Khomeini's own power base. The White House also lacked accurate information about the [Iranian] military—the factions within the army and the degree to which the military leadership would remain loyal to the shah."[46]

Moreover, he adds, the administration failed in a major prediction. They suspected that Khomeini might disappear quickly from the political stage following an ouster of the shah, and that the moderate Mehdi Bazargan, whom Khomeini would install as the head of a provisional government, would preside over a new, "American-friendly" regime. Such a benign outcome would not come to pass.

Mohsen M. Milani depicts a Carter administration in troubling disarray. "There seemed to have been at least four different U.S. centers of decision making during Iran's revolutionary movement: the White House, the State Department, the National Security Council, and the U.S. Embassy in Teheran," he writes. "Their analysis of the turmoil and their proposed strategies of action often differed from one another. All four centers made flawed judgments about the shah's regime and its opponents. None seemed to have understood the dynamics of Iran's revolutionary movement or its cultural and religious heritage—prerequisites to formulating sound policy.

"In short, the United States did not speak with one voice when, more than at any other time, unanimity of action was essential. If the contradictory policies of the U.S. administration were not a calculated move to undermine the shah, as has been suggested by some Iranian monarchists, then one can only conclude that [the] U.S. foreign policy establishment has no appropriate mechanism to deal with revolutionary crises. . . . Considering the abundance of resources available to the United States in Iran, its 'loss of Iran' should be viewed as a masterpiece of flawed diplomacy."[47]

While the Carter administration sleepwalked and equivocated through the gathering disaster that would end his long reign, the shah himself was torn by indecision. Taking action that would produce a massacre in the streets of Tehran was not an option for a man who sought to be remembered as a benevolent monarch, not a ruthless dictator. After he fled his country for exile in Egypt in January 1979, he reflected:

> I am told today that I should have applied martial law more forcefully. This would have cost my

country less dear than the bloody anarchy now established there. But a sovereign cannot save his throne by spilling blood of his fellow-countrymen. A dictator can do it because he acts in the name of an ideology which he believes he must make triumphant, no matter what the price. A sovereign is not a dictator. There is between him and his people an alliance which he cannot break. A dictator has nothing to pass on: power belongs to him and him alone. A sovereign receives a crown. I could envisage my son mounting the throne in my own lifetime.[48]

No such succession would occur. The long reign of the Pahlavis was over. Exuberant crowds greeted Ayatollah Ruhollah Khomeini's entrance into Tehran on February 1, 1979. Iran's history, and indeed the world's, was about to take a new, ominous, and violent turn. Wrote Brzezinski, "Iranian history after the fall of the shah tells us eloquently how viable any contrived coalition [government in Iran] would have been: the successors to the shah spent the subsequent months in literally killing one another, in widespread executions, in repeated and increasingly murderous assassinations, in an intensifying civil war."[49]

The world and Iran still suffer from the effects of the Islamic revolution that dethroned the shah. Khomeini and his followers sensed that the shah was weak—and that, by extension, so was the Carter administration, paralyzed by a human rights policy that it sought to apply to a foreign policy challenge whose consequences it couldn't begin to understand.

The visage of the shah adorned Iran's currency until the Khomeini-led revolution forced the longtime monarch into exile and brought an end to the Pahlavi dynasty.

With Tehran's Shayad (Shah Memorial) landmark in the background, jubilant supporters of Ayatollah Khomeini celebrated his triumphant return to Iran on February 1, 1979.

En route to Tehran and a resumption of his rule, the shah boarded a plane in Rome in August 1953, after a counter-coup overthrew the opponent, Mohammed Mossadeq, who had briefly unseated him and forced him to flee the country.

With the U.S. invasion of Iraq in March 2003 imminent, followers of Osama bin Laden and Pakistani religious parties demonstrated in Karachi, some chanting "America is the terrorist."

Inspirational posters bearing the image of Ayatollah Ruhollah Khomeini abounded in Tehran in the aftermath of the historic revolution that deposed the long-ruling shah.

Amid the mountainous terrain of the Jagdalak region, Afghan mujahidin prepared their weapons in anticipation of an attack by Soviet troops in February 1987.

Chapter 3

Carter, the Revolution, and the Aftermath

The shah was on the verge of leaving Iran for the last time. The date was December 27, 1978; he would be gone in 20 days. In feckless pronouncements, the Carter administration publicly stated its hope that he "would continue to play an important role" in leading Iran to the formation of a new government of "national reconciliation." How this would be possible without support from Washington was unclear. Apart from offering such tepid communiqués, Washington crawled at the pace of a holiday slowdown. "There is no air of crisis in the Carter administration," the *New York Times* reported. "Carter remained at Camp David, where he had been mixing pleasure with work all week." Meanwhile, Secretary of Defense Harold Brown flew to California for a holiday. "Zbigniew Brzezinski," the *Times* report added, "was also not at work today."[1]

What conclusions could be drawn? From the shah's perspective, there could be no mistaking the reports he was following in the press. The message was painfully clear:

though he had enjoyed working relationships with American presidents for nearly 40 years, the Iranian crisis—his crisis—was not deemed important enough to keep the American foreign policy team awake at the switch. He thought he deserved a better fate—both from his own people and his American allies. [2]

"As it turned out, the United States offered no help," says historian Manoucher Ganji. "Instead it often spoke with multiple voices to a distraught shah. From George Ball and Zbigniew Brzezinski to Cyrus Vance to Jimmy Carter and William Sullivan, each offered a different bit of advice."[3] As it turned out, its wishy-washy policies were as much a cause of the success of the revolution as any other factor.

This was yet another juncture—a third stage—that cried out for Washington's involvement. Not only did the administration lack a grand strategy for dealing with Iran immediately before and after its revolution, but even as the monarchy's demise was imminent, Jimmy Carter presented no plan to the shah. Nor had contact been made with the likely architects of a new government. The American president had no shortage of counsel—from the State Department and Ambassador Sullivan, coupled with strong urgings from Israel and France—but none of that advice held sway. Instead, unbelievably, the United States drifted in isolation while a country with which it had enjoyed friendly relations for nearly four decades was lost to a revolutionary movement profoundly hostile to U.S. interests.

* * *

When the shah fled his country on January 16, 1979, signs of the preceding, yearlong turmoil abounded.

Remnants of the fallen monarchy were visible everywhere, manifest in shattered glass, discarded leaflets, shops in ruin. Tehran was a city in chaos and distress. One man triumphantly held up a copy of the newspaper *Kayhan*. The headline read "Shah Raft" or "The Shah Is Gone." Some Iranians ignited fires with photographs of the shah, while others cut his picture out of bank notes. One bronze statue of Reza Shah, his father, was yanked down and destroyed; the head of another became a makeshift soccer ball.

In several cities the military stepped in, killing and wounding a number of citizens. But in Tehran, neither troops from the 400,000- man army nor members of the police force were capable of suppressing the popular rebellion that spread throughout the city. [4]

Ayatollah Khomeini had seized control of the incipient revolution a full year before he returned to Iran on February 1, 1979. Although he had lived in exile for 14 years, Khomeini still enjoyed a large following among Islamic seminarians. From his home in Neauphle-le-Chateau, a tiny village in France, Khomeini would emerge twice a day, his supporters screaming *Allahu Akbar* ("God is great"). Even from afar he orchestrated protests in Iran, his lectures disseminated via cassette tapes to mosques throughout Tehran.[5]

The exiled ayatollah appealed to various segments of Iran's population. His frequent references to the "disinherited" (*mustadafeen*) resonated with student radicals, Marxists, and Shiites alike. Shortly before his expulsion from Iran in 1964, he had attracted notice by publicly condemning both the shah's violations of the constitution and the granting of extraterritoriality to American civilian and military advisers and their dependents. "You have extirpated the very roots of our independence," he wrote from Najaf in 1967, scolding Prime Minister Hoveida. He denounced the United States as "the head of the imperialist serpent," accused multinational corporations of looting Iran's resources, and deplored Iran's "domination" by foreign capital and the squandering of public funds in massive arms purchases.

At the outbreak of the uprising in January 1978, Khomeini exhorted dissidents to pursue their struggle until they had deposed the shah. Disregarding many of his advisers, he insisted that the battle be waged without recourse to arms, declaring that the Shiite faith would prevail over brute force. His calculation proved well-founded: a year later, the imperial army—the most powerful in the Middle East after that of Israel—succumbed to "bare-handed revolutionaries" who suffered tens of thousands of casualties en route to their victory.[6]

The climactic Jaleh Square confrontation in Tehran in September made matters between the monarchy and the religious opposition irreconcilable. Ayatollah Shariatmadari, a leading religious figure in Qum, predicted during the first week of September that the government would collapse in three months if it did not meet the demands of the religious leaders.[7] Demonstrations continued apace, with general strikes occurring thereafter. By November 1978, workers in the oil industry, the customs department, government factories, banks, and newspapers had gone on strike, ultimately paralyzing the economy.

But neither the widespread discontent with the monarchy nor Khomeini's singular ability to rouse the masses as a populist leader can fully explain the events that galvanized the shah's opponents during his final year on the throne. Rather, the success of Khomeini's revolution must be considered in terms of Shiite theology. "The rise of the Shi'ite clergy is rooted in the history and ideology of Shi'ism," wrote Eric Rouleau.[8]

This ideology held that justice would not prevail in the Muslim community until the "great occultation" (as the Twelfth Imam's disappearance is known) ended with his return to earth (resurrection). Thus for Shiites, every ruler —or ruling party—is necessarily a usurper, since through the very act of ruling one is substituting himself for the Twelfth Imam, who alone is empowered to execute the divine will. This conviction has led the Shiite clergy to contest the authority and actions of the various dynasties that have governed Persia, and especially to oppose a royal power whenever it has opened Iran to foreign influences that might "pervert" Islam or introduce customs that conflict with Muslim culture and tradition.

In this vein, Shiites would have opposed the shah's rule even if he had been a benevolent monarch. By seeking to introduce "Western" reforms and thus "corrupt" Islamic culture, the shah was bound to be regarded as a usurper. Iran's Shiite clerics continually spoke out against social injustice, moral decay, and corruption—code phrases referring to the Peacock Throne and its American advisers. The panacea for these ills, they said, was a determined march backward—a return to Islam's roots as "a way of defending the national virtue and identity against the rape by Western technology."[9]

The ayatollah knew that the shah, in a spirit of penitence and conciliation, had already admitted his past errors on television and permitted the arrests of many high-ranking government officials. Khomeini also knew in December 1978 that the monarch was ready to make more radical concessions. The shah had invited National Front leader Karim Sanjabi to the royal palace, where he offered Sanjabi the opportunity to administer the government. But Sanjabi refused, citing his agreement with Khomeini that the shah was not a legitimate ruler. The shah then offered the prime ministership to another member of the National Front, Shapour Bhaktiar, an opponent of the radical clerics, who was committed instead to a constitutional transfer of power. One of the conditions of Bhaktiar's acceptance was that the shah would leave the country on a "vacation" of indeterminate duration.

As prime minister, Bhaktiar promptly disbanded SAVAK and granted greater freedom to the press. For the sake of maintaining order, he asked Khomeini not to return to Iran right away, fearing that the Ayatollah's arrival might incite a military coup. Khomeini, ever a master of public relations, acquiesced, announcing a postponement of his return at a news conference in France on January 25.

A furious protest followed in Iran. Attempting to storm police headquarters on January 28, rioters were shot down by army and police marksmen stationed on rooftops. In two days of bloody riots, touched off when airports were closed to prevent the ayatollah's return, 37 demonstrators were killed and more than 200 wounded. It was later learned that a number of the shah's generals, notably Amir-Hosein Rabii, the commander of the air force, had devised a plan to shoot down Khomeini's plane. Another option, included in the same plan, was to divert the plane to a remote part of Iran where the ayatollah would be placed under arrest. Seeking U.S. approval, the generals apprised Brzezinski of the plan. The national security adviser relayed the information to Carter, but the president "wouldn't have anything to do with it," Brzezinski recalled.[10]

The moderate Bhaktiar possessed little political lever-age. He was unable to persuade Khomeini to delay his ar-rival further, in the face of overwhelming popular support for his return to Iran. Just three days after the shah's depar-ture, a million people marched in Tehran, demanding Bhak-tiar's resignation. On February 1, the 76-year-old Khomeini returned, declaring that through his Islamic Revolution a true Islamic republic would be established. He appointed his own prime minister, Mehdi Barzagan. The Bhaktiar government collapsed within ten days and was replaced by the revolutionary forces.

The time was suddenly ripe for Khomeini to announce the establishment of an Islamic state.

The charismatic cleric was wildly popular. Some of his most fervent—perhaps feverish—followers even swore that they had seen the face of Khomeini—the *sayyid*, or de-scendant of the prophet —etched on the surface of the moon.[11] He had captured the imagination of the most dis-parate groups—intellectuals, religious fundamentalists, ba-zaar merchants, the urban masses—all of whom embraced his prescriptions for the creation of an Islamic state.

Throughout 1978 he had enunciated several objec-tives. First, all protests against the monarchy must continue. Second, the protests would end only with the overthrow of the shah. Third, compromise with the monarch was not an option. Fourth and last, the establishment of an "Islamic" government was the goal of the entire movement.

When the shah's government began to make conces-sions in late 1978, Khomeini was unrelenting. "The Iranian nation will not be fooled," he said. "It will not overlook the real criminal." By opening Iran's resources to foreigners, the shah had revealed himself as "a traitor and a rebel." Not only did the nation, from "east to west, from north to south, abhor the shah," but the monarchy was a "treason to Islam and the nation."

The shah had destroyed the economy, giving away the country's oil to the United States and other industrial powers, charged Khomeini. He had reduced his nation's economic productivity in order to provide a healthier market for American goods. Iran's military had been rendered subordinate to foreign leadership. The shah had also ruthlessly suppressed freedom of expression and massacred thousands of dissenters, asserted the ayatollah, albeit without confirmation of any kind by the press. [12]

Both the shah and Carter were referred to as Yazid, or agents of Satan. "All the problems of Iran," the ayatollah elaborated, "are the work of America." A Western reporter interviewed Khomeini about his own intentions late in 1978, as the end of the shah's rule seemed near. What would be the ayatollah's position in an Islamic republic? "I will not have any position in the future government," was Khomeini's coy reply. "I will not be the President or the Prime Minister. I will be some sort of supervisor of their activities. I will give them guidance. If I see some deviation or mistake, I will remind them how to correct it." When asked how the new system of government would work, he grew irritated, saying, "I've already answered your question."[13]

He responded similarly to other questions. "We are for an Islamic system, that is, a democratic regime founded on popular consensus and Islamic law," Khomeini said. About his own acceptance of a position in the new regime, he averred, "My age, my religious position, and my inclinations are against it."[14] In truth, Khomeini's ambiguous replies to the question about what form his Islamic government might take had the effect of uniting all segments of Iranian society, leading them to believe that they could join forces as activist opponents of the former monarchy.

Khomeini's aides fostered the impression that once the revolution was in place, the ayatollah would return to Qum and leave the workings of government to the secular technocrats. The ayatollah exerted masterly control over the press, to which he granted frequent interviews.

"There was a committee who read Khomeini all the questions, and would discuss the answers with him," former Iranian President Abolhassan Bani-Sadr later revealed. "During [an] interview, sometimes the interpreter would fill out the phrases on his behalf." Thus the media often disseminated a distorted impression of Khomeini and of his conception of an Islamic republic.

Ayatollah Khomeini's return to Iran on January 31, 1979, is often referred to as the second phase of the revolution. For the West and Iran, it was the beginning of the unknown. Inside Iran it would be hard to imagine that an unlikely admixture of Marxists, nationalists, Shiites, Kurds and others could coexist under the banner of Islam, which itself comprised rightist, leftist, and centrist factions. Even the Shiite clergy was divided, despite its avowed allegiance to Khomeini.

Despite Khomeini's rigidity, in the early stages of the revolution he appointed people to official posts who gave the revolutionary movement an appearance of openness and tolerance. Even before he returned from exile, he named a Westernized liberal, Mehdi Bazargan, as his prime minister and asked him to form a cabinet. Within a fortnight the monarchy fell, and it was Bazargan who led the first Islamic government. But in a harbinger of things to come, a shadowy, clerically dominated Revolutionary Council ruled alongside Bazargan's cabinet, setting up makeshift revolutionary courts and often enacting laws on its own authority.

The interplay of Bazargan and the clerics was delicate. It was Bazargan's design to preserve the instruments of power created under the shah, resist nationalization, pursue an open foreign policy with all nations, and destroy burgeoning revolutionary bodies that had begun to usurp power. But his aims ran counter to Khomeini's. In Bazargan's incisive view, until the revolution Khomeini's strategy had been "to serve Iran through Islam," but after gaining power it became "serving Islam through Iran."[15]

Khomeini ignored Bazargan's complaints, tantrums, and threats to resign. In the end Bazargan was forced out. To the ayatollah's followers, the prime minister's crimes were manifold: he had opposed the swift, secret trials and executions of Old Regime leftovers, criticized the Islamic constitution as undemocratic, and tried to normalize relations with the United States. He would resign two days after the American hostages were seized in November 1979, condemned by the student militants holding the embassy for "sitting down at the table with the wolf," as Brzezinski remarked at a conference in Algiers. Said Bazargan, "I was always the last to know what was going on. I found myself at a dead end."[16]

Meanwhile, the Carter administration remained disorganized and out of touch with unfolding events in Iran nearly a month after the shah's departure. "While the masses were celebrating the victory of the revolution and

destroying every visible symbol of the Pahlavi dynasty, including the shah's statues in the cities, Washington was still
pondering its predicament in Iran," historian Mohsen Milani recalled.[17]

Following the shah's exile, "Bazargan's government
worked arduously to lay the foundation for strong bilateral
ties between Iran and the United States based on reciproc-
ity and mutual respect." U.S. policy toward the Bazargan
regime was an uncoordinated failure, Milani continues:
"Was the real objective of U.S. policy to support Bazargan's provisional government, which it identified as moderate? Was the objective to open a dialogue with the fundamentalists? Was it to undermine the Islamic Revolution?
Was it to avoid intervening in Iran's internal affairs by supporting neither the provisional government nor the government in order to leave open the option of developing
relations with whoever emerged victorious? Whatever the
real objectives, the U.S. policy alienated both the fundamentalists and the provisional government and contributed
to the consolidation of power by the fundamentalists."[18]

A tantalizing question arises: If the Carter administration's "contradictory policies" weren't intended to subvert
the shah (as some Iranian monarchists have maintained),
one must conclude that "[the] U.S. foreign policy establishment has no appropriate mechanism to deal with revolutionary crises," Milani suggests.[19]

"The Carter administration maintained quiet channels
of communication with Bazargan and his aides," says analyst Robin Wright. Still, the administration "avoided" or
"ignored" dealing with many of the key mullahs and revolutionary organizations. More damning still, "There is no
known record of any meeting between American political

or intelligence emissaries and Khomeini, either when he was in exile or after his return to Iran. The United States consistently failed to deal directly with him or what he represented."[20] With no penetration into the world of Khomeini and his supporters, what realistic chance did Washington have of influencing events in Iran before or after the revolution?

Despite the efforts of moderates like Barzagan, the systemic intolerance of the revolutionary movement was soon evident. Turbaned mullahs and bearded revolutionaries were ubiquitous. In time, the pace of change ushered in by the new revolution would cause a massive upheaval. Some 500,000 Iranians—mostly middle class and professional—left the country to find a better life abroad.

Bazargan had voiced sound ideas about how to govern. "I avoid haste and extremes," he said. "I am given to careful study and gradualism. I was this way in the past and will not change my approach in the future."[21] This stance left the 72-year-old moderate squarely at odds with the ideologically unyielding Khomeini, whose radical agenda would prevail, leaving the official government, as Bazargan ruefully put it, like a "knife without a blade."[22]

The ultimate irony had surfaced—those who had protested against the shah's rule and forced him into exile would themselves tolerate no protest. By 1980, the Islamic Republican Party would control the executive, legislative, and judicial branches of government and all of the news media. Other political parties were suppressed. Candidates for election had to be approved by a Council of Guardians. Support for the Islamic Republic was the *sine qua non* for candidacy, as it was for key positions in government, education, and other sectors of society. Criticism of Ayatollah

Khomeini or of the government's ideological foundation would not be tolerated.

The Carter administration had cause to wonder how it could once have viewed the eccentric ayatollah as somehow preferable to the shah. Khomeini had clearly delineated his concept of an Islamic government. His ideas had been largely ignored, but now they were being enacted with a vengeance.

In his first interview from exile, the shah was asked by David Frost whether the United States had provided him with useful advice before the revolution forced him to flee. The deposed monarch answered, "The United States should have assessed the situation. The results are here. Is the world satisfied with what is going on in Iran? Let them [the United States] decide if this [Khomeini's regime] is better than before."[23]

In exile in Egypt, the shah held out hope that he would be somehow recalled to Tehran to resume the throne, as he had been in 1953. Ambassador Sullivan, however, informed Washington that "these wishful thoughts were pure moonshine . . . we should instead be preparing ourselves for the fact that the revolution was going to succeed and . . .we need to accommodate ourselves to it in the most effective way in order to protect United States national interests."[24]

For his troubles Sullivan received "a most unpleasant and abrasive cable from Washington," which, in his judgment, "contained an unacceptable aspersion upon my loyalty," he recalled.

Meanwhile, Khomeini set about consolidating clerical rule under his leadership. His authoritarianism provoked the opposition of the secular nationalist and left-wing elements that had supported his revolution, but they were no match for the hold he had gained over the Iranian people. In fact, the most determined opposition to his rule came from more senior Islamic clerics who challenged his religious authority.

But their dissent counted for little. Khomeini possessed political genius, which they lacked. He based his rule on the doctrine of *velayat-e faqih,* or "government of the Islamist jurist." The doctrine holds that a true Islamic state must be based on the Koran and modeled after the Prophet's Islamic community of the seventh century; it should be administered by the clerical class, who are the Prophet's heirs. As the self-appointed governing Islamic jurist, Khomeini wielded power over the regime's president and prime minister and the elected members of its parliament, all of whom held offices provided for in the new Islamic constitution.

Under his authority, the educational system was purged of non-Islamic influences. Squads of young Muslim militiamen enforced a strict Islamic code of conduct. Educated Iranian women, who had reached an advanced stage of emancipation before the revolution, had their role in public life sharply curtailed and were required to envelop their heads and bodies in Islamic dress whenever they appeared in public.

The success of the Khomeini revolution and its declared desire to export itself caused grave alarm among Iran's Arab neighbors, especially Iraq. With its prevailing secular, pan-Arabist ideology and a large but politically marginalized Shiite population, Iraq was a vulnerable target. Tehran-based broadcasts poured hatred and contempt on the Iraq regime and called on the Iraqi people to overthrow it.

* * *

Some have argued that Carter could have done nothing to save the shah. The facts suggest otherwise. Through a series of missed opportunities and clumsy responses to unfolding events, the Carter administration all but sealed the shah's fate and assured the installation of a revolutionary government whose hostility to the United States was a matter of historical record.

As Pierre Salinger sagely points out, the situation facing the Carter administration was not a case of either/or:

> The choice was not, as some have portrayed it, solely between the shah and the Ayatollah Khomeini. There were other alternatives, which, if backed by the United States early enough, could have produced a moderate government not hostile to the United States. Let us state it bluntly: the Carter administration didn't know what to do about Iran. And this indecision led directly to November 4, 1979, the day the hostages were seized. In the fateful months of the shah's waning rule over what would soon be transformed from America's strongest ally in the region to its bitterest enemy, United States policy ran down two widely diverging paths.[25]

While Salinger did not weigh the long-term consequences of the administration's Iran blunder (his book was published in 1981), he revealed the inner workings of an administration whose policies were doomed to failure.

The State Department, led by Secretary Vance, advocated a policy of constructive contact with the Iranian opposition. In direct contrast, Brzezinski, the national security adviser, urged the administration to support the shah staunchly against his opponents. These diametrically opposed positions precluded the formulation of a single, coherent policy and brought the administration's dealings with Iran to a virtual standstill.

Having served under Presidents Kennedy and Johnson, Cyrus Vance well knew the damage that an unpopular conflict like the Vietnam War could inflict on an administration. Vance thus remained noncommittal on the question of backing the shah and assuring Iran of U.S. military support if necessary. Brzezinski had been shaped by a different experience. Polish born, he had married the niece of Eduard Benes, a Czech leader overthrown by the communists after World War II. His approach to foreign policy was often confrontational. A fierce anticommunist, Brzezinski invariably favored a hard line when dealing with the nation's adversaries.[26]

Had Carter possessed either strong views on what to do about Iran or considerable experience in foreign policy, the tendencies of Vance and Brzezinski to pull in opposite directions might have been less counterproductive. But Carter entered office with negligible experience in foreign affairs beyond some work for the Trilateral Commission, where his relationship with Vance and Brzezinski—who would become his mentors, rather than vice versa—began to develop.[27] "If he had set out deliberately to do so, Jimmy Carter could not have constructed a situation in which two opposing forces would pull more strongly on his ambivalent center," writes Salinger.[28]

Thus when the Iran crisis commenced in the summer of 1978, the Carter administration was ill-prepared to re-

spond. It had failed to recognize that the shah's reign was
faltering and that, in the gathering atmosphere of revolution, the U.S. embassy in Tehran was vulnerable. The embassy would be overrun by militants 16 months later.

The Iranian monarch, who so often had been accused
of countenancing brutality, was now ordering his troops to
fire their guns harmlessly into the air, thus emboldening
the protestors who massed in demonstrations against him.
The shah may have once had the stomach to effect a military solution to his problems, but now, ill and withdrawn,
he would not permit his generals to use force. Mirroring
the shah's own ineffectiveness was the Carter administration's inability to act decisively. This inability to influence
events in any manner beneficial to the United States would
persist after the shah's departure, through the formation of
the constitution of the Islamic Republic of Iran.

* * *

A story goes that the day before Khomeini returned to
Tehran, a local writer urged him to forget the idea of an
"Islamic" republic and opt for "a republic, pure and simple" instead. It is unknown whether Khomeini answered
the man directly. But a month later he spoke in Qum and
gave an implicit answer. "What the nation wants," he said,
"is an Islamic republic; not just a republic, not a democratic
republic. Do not use the term 'democratic.' That is the
Western style."[29] This sentiment conflicted with a statement he had made in November 1978, when he insisted
that the goal of the revolution was "an Islamic republic
which would protect the independence and democracy of
Iran." Now he claimed that democracy was "alien to Islam."

Not a month later, Iran's voting population, including everyone aged 16 and older, cast ballots on the question of whether to replace the monarchy with an Islamic republic. The opposition—including the National Democratic Front, the *Fadayan*, and seven Kurdish groups—boycotted the referendum. The *Mojahedin* declared their "conditional" approval of the measure, but other groups—Bazargan's Iran Freedom Movement, Sanjabi's National Front, and Shariatmadari's Islamic People's Republican Party—joined the Tudeh and the Islamic Republican Party in urging a "yes" vote. An overwhelming 98.2-percent majority favored an Islamic state.

When a draft of the constitution drew criticism from secular quarters, Khomeini, speaking in June to a delegation of clerics, urged his listeners to read the document from an "Islamic perspective" and defend its tenets when "foreign intellectuals" and others without "faith in Islam" expressed critical views. Islamic parties followed his advice and offered their critique of the draft at the Congress of Muslim Critics of the Constitution. Another draft was distributed by Ayatollah Hosain-Ali Montazeri. Together, the drafts sought to enshrine Islam as the basis of the constitution, as well as of the judiciary and the family in Iranian society.[30]

Delegates to the congress advocated endorsement of the "twelver" Shiite version of Islam and the adoption of a provision requiring that the republic's president and prime minister be practicing Shiites who were versed in Islamic law. In addition, they demanded a right of veto over all laws and the right of Islamic jurists to appoint judges, supervise the judiciary, and approve presidential candidates. They rejected the notion of equality between men and women, noting specifically that under Islamic law women could not serve as judges or governors. Sovereignty, they maintained, belongs only to God and, through him, to the Prophet, the imams, and the jurists. In Islam, one speaker at the congress asserted, sovereignty does not belong to "the people"; to be governed by "God's law" must be the general condition.

Abolhassan Bani-Sadr was the first president appointed by Khomeini. Like Bazargan, Bani-Sadr provided an ongoing counterpoint to the concept of an Islamic government advanced by Khomeini and the clerics. Anti-authoritarian by nature, Bani-Sadr contended that an Islamic state ought to be free of formal structures and that power in such a state should be relatively diffuse. In his ideal version of an Islamic state, each individual would be free to interpret the divine law for himself. In such a democratic setting there would be no need for a final authority or object of emulation.

But Ayatollah Beheshti, the leader of the Islamic Republican Party, argued that support for Bani-Sadr must be conditional upon his pursuing a militant Islamic path. From the standpoint of the Islamic constitution, the "president counts for nothing," said Beheshti.[31]

The United States made little attempt to influence events in Iran; based on its policies, Washington seemed indifferent. One measure of this evident disinterest was the matter of the shah's admittance to the United States. In exile the shah went first to Egypt, then to the Bahamas and on to Mexico. One doctor diagnosed him as having cancer of the spleen and blood. The disease had been controlled with medicine for years, but now a tumor appeared on his neck and his doctors believed that he should be treated in New York.

But the shah did not want to go to the United States. "I've never gone where I'm not welcome," he explained.[32] Indeed, arrangements had been made for him to stay at an enclosed estate in Rancho Mirage, California. But as he awaited word in Egypt, he suspected the United States did not want him to come, as demonstrations had been linked to his pending entry. After he had stayed in Morocco for nearly two months, where demonstrations against him took place at universities, King Hassan politely requested that he leave. Now the shah asked U.S. officials point blank if he could go to the United States. Again the government balked, citing unstable conditions in Iran that might jeopardize Americans living there if the shah were admitted to the United States.

The shah's twin sister, Princess Ashraf, pressed his case with a personal missive to Carter on August 10, 1979. She explained that the shah wished to establish residency in the United States, where he might find an appropriate place for his family to live and his children to be educated. She also wrote, as if to remind the president, "One of the best-known traditions of the United States throughout the world has been its record of hospitality and refuge to those who are forced to leave their own countries for political reasons." On the dangers of admitting her brother to the country she said, "I believe at one time that your government was concerned over the possible harm to American citizens in Iran which might result from his being given refuge (in the United States). I do not believe that cause for this continues to exist." Her letter closed with this declaration: "I cannot believe that means could not be taken by your country to assume the essential safety of the United States citizens in Iran, rather than to submit to any such type of blackmail."[33] Her last statement alluded precisely to the overriding problem: Even prior to the hostage affair, which was still three months in the future, the Carter administration was allowing Iran's revolutionaries to dictate the terms of the countries' bilateral relationship. Improbably and outrageously, the tail was wagging the dog.

A week later, Secretary of State Warren Christopher —by this time Vance had resigned—replied to the Princess on behalf of the president, noting the "unsettled" situation in Iran and how popular emotions "ran high." Nonetheless, the administration expected that that relations between Iran and the United States had "a reasonable chance" to improve in the near future. We are still "reviewing our position" on the "best timing of your brother's move to the United States," he said.[34]

Soon after Christopher's letter arrived at the Princess's townhouse, Robert Armao, the shah's assistant, quickly surmised that it was "a thank-you-but-no-thank-you" response. Learning of the brush-off by the United States, the shah made plans to seek medical treatment in Mexico. "I do not want to go to the States," he said, overruling aides who doubted that he would receive adequate treatment in Mexico. "It will be nothing but problems for me." Finally, Mexican friends prevailed on the shah to go to the United States, where he would undoubtedly receive the best treatment available.[35]

The decision to admit the shah was finally made on October 19, 1979, at Carter's weekly Friday morning foreign policy breakfast. The consensus held that some risk was involved, but the U.S. government owed the shah this consideration, given his shabby treatment in recent months by American officials who suggested that he was not welcome in their country.[36]

Carter shared this view. He polled those present at the breakfast: Vice-President Walter Mondale, Vance, Brzezinski, Secretary of Defense Brown, and White House chief of staff Hamilton Jordan. They unanimously believed that the shah should be allowed to enter the United States. Carter then asked, portentously, "What are you guys going to recommend that we do when they take our embassy and hold our people hostage?"[37]

Despite the efforts to preserve its secrecy, the shah's departure from Mexico on October 22 was leaked to the press. The following day some 30,000 Iranians marched past the U.S. embassy in Tehran, screaming and waving their fists. Among the protestors were members of the radical Society of Islamic Students.[38]

Students had been united since the departure of the shah nine months earlier and had become the militant accomplices of Ayatollah Khomeini. The students decided to organize a demonstration for November 4 to protest the latest obstacle in returning the shah to Iran to stand trial on charges that he had stolen money from the country and tortured his political opposition. November 4 was chosen because it would be the first anniversary of an invasion of the campus of Teheran University by Iranian soldiers, who had killed several students in the process.

Of the events that preceded the November 4, 1979 seizure of the embassy and taking of 66 American hostages, the most provocative to many Iranians was the October 22, 1979 admission of the shah to a New York hospital for medical treatment. The shah recalled this episode in his autobiography, *Answer to History*.

During my stay in New York Hospital there was little contact with the U.S. Administration. President Carter never phoned or sent a message, neither did any other high U.S. official. . . . On November 8, I publicly expressed my willingness to leave the United States in hopes of freeing the Americans being held hostage. However, my doctor's position was that any travel for me at that time could well be fatal.[39]

The shah recalled that by the end of November "the U.S. wanted me out of their country at almost any cost." His next stop would be Panama. After it had been decided that he would depart, President Carter called the shah, expressing warm wishes. "It was the first and only time I had spoken with the president since wishing him farewell on New Year's Day 1978 when he visited Tehran," said the shah, who left the United States on the morning of December 15, with "the American promises [of support in Panama] still ringing in my ears."[40]

Mohsen Milani notes that the embassy takeover was "yet another illustration of the insensitivity or perhaps ignorance of U.S. policymakers about the dynamics of Iran's internal politics." It is beyond dispute, he says, that the event created "a hysterical anti-U.S. climate in Iran."[41]

Dissent and inconsistency characterized the Carter administration's deliberations about admitting the shah, with the president and his advisers apparently aware of the possible repercussions of doing so. Brzezinski favored the action as a demonstration of "our strength and loyalty to an old friend, even if it means personal danger to a group of very vulnerable Americans." L. Bruce Laingen, the U.S. chargé d'affaires in Tehran, had urged that such a move be delayed because it could result in the takeover of the embassy and the seizure of hostages.[42]

In the weeks before the takeover, leftists opposed to the Bazargan government had organized multiple demonstrations against U.S. imperialism in the neighborhood of the embassy. Students following the Imam's Line, a group of militant Islamic students who also opposed the provisional government and were outraged by the shah's admission to the United States, spearheaded the embassy's seizure. Upon entering the embassy grounds the group's spiritual leader, Sheikholislam Mussavi Khoeiniha, called immediately to inform Khomeini of the action, ignoring the provisional government. While Khomeini did not initially support the takeover, he soon recognized its potential benefits, deeming it "Iran's second revolution, more important than the first one."[43]

The students' defiance of Bazargan's demand that they release the American hostages immediately demonstrated the ineffectuality of his government, and he resigned two days after the takeover. "The hostage ordeal brought to the core of Iranian politics some of the most radical elements of the fundamentalist camp and suffocated the moderate elements," says Milani.[44]

The seizure of American diplomats as hostages in Tehran not only sounded the death knell of the Bazargan government, but also brought into the open the conflict between Iran and the United States. Khomeini had not forgiven the seven U.S. presidents who over 30 years had unfailingly supported the dictator most Iranians considered Mohammed Reza Pahlavi to be. The shah's admission to the United States in October 1979 confirmed Khomeini's suspicions that the U.S. administration sought to return the fallen monarch to his throne. The American gesture, praised as "humanitarian" and "courageous" in the West, was perceived in Teheran as a new and intolerable provocation.[45]

Khomeini made masterful use of widespread anti-American feelings to mobilize the population under his banner. The occupation of the American embassy thus came at the perfect time, uniting nationalists, Marxists, and Islamists. The takeover was trumpeted as a victory over a "nest of spies." With the publication of the embassy's secret files, contacts between the United States and Iranian liberals were exposed. This provided an impetus for new trials and executions. Khomeini would react similarly after Carter's abortive hostage rescue mission of April 25, 1980; the United States, even in failure, offered Khomeini tangible evidence that the principal threat to the Iranian people was foreign intervention.[46]

With the resignation of Bazargan, the "third stage" of the revolution could begin. Now the Islamic Republic could begin the work of purging Western elements calling for liberalization. Khomeini could now use the hostage crisis to separate the "good" from the "evil" within the society. Those who supported the Islamic students in their seizure of the embassy were in the good camp, i.e., against imperialism and for the revolution. All others were deemed "nationalists" and consequently reviled as "Westernized liberals" who were disposed to "compromise with imperialism."

Indeed, they could safely be labeled pro-Western counterrevolutionaries. In this light it is hardly surprising that few Iranians dared publicly to take a stand against the embassy's occupation.[46] Moderate parties and public figures generally remained silent or diffident, lest they accused of defending the United States. Only the president, Bani-Sadr, had the courage—some would say imprudence —to state, on November 6, 1979, that he disapproved of the seizure of hostages both on Islamic moral grounds and in the interest of the revolution. He frequently reiterated his opposition, and his relationship with Ayatollah Khomeini predictably deteriorated.

All the while, according to one historian, "The Carter administration pursued a self-defeating and inconsistent policy toward Iran." This assessment continued, "When [Carter] did focus on Iran, his record was one of oscillation between the two factions [in his administration]."[47]

By now it was abundantly clear that Carter's emphasis on a human rights-based foreign policy alone may have contributed to what was to follow and had collided with the preservation of U.S. strategic interests in the Persian Gulf region. By failing to protect those interests, the Carter administration supervised the demise of the crucial relationship that the shah and his father had carefully nurtured for decades. Mohsen Milani sheds light on the disarray that afflicted the Carter White House: "There seemed to have been at least four different U.S. centers of decision making during Iran's revolutionary movement: the White House, the State Department, the National Security Council, and the U.S. Embassy in Tehran. Their analyses of the turmoil and their proposed strategies of action often differed from one another. All four centers made flawed judgments about the shah's regime and its opponents."[48] None seemed to have understood the dynamics of Iran's revolutionary movement or its cultural and religious heritage—prerequisites for the formulation of sound policy.

In short, the United States did not speak with one voice when, more than ever, clarity and decisiveness were essential. If the contradictory policies of the administration did not amount to a calculated move to undermine the shah, as has been suggested by some Iranian monarchists, one can only conclude that the U.S. foreign policy establishment had no appropriate mechanism for managing revolutionary crises. "The shah's exile marked the end of the short period when the United States was the dominant foreign power in Iran (1953–1979)," Milani writes. "Considering the abundance of resources available to the United States in Iran, its 'loss of Iran' would be viewed as a masterpiece of flawed diplomacy."[49]

At New York Hospital, the shah received the message that the embassy had been taken. His first reaction spoke volumes. What surprised him was not that the event had occurred, but that the U.S. position in Iran had become so impotent that a band of radical students would undertake such a bold action. The students, like others in Iran, had concluded that the Carter administration was weak. "My people are like children," the shah said. "If you let them take one piece of candy and you don't scold them, they'll take another and another until they soon have the whole bowl. And that's exactly what happened. They perceived the Carter administration to be so weak that they could just slap it and slap it and slap it."[50]

When Carter learned of the embassy takeover, he and his foreign policy team deliberated about whom to consult inside Iran's government. Presumably, their best contacts were the prime minister, Bazargan, and the foreign minister, Ibrahim Yazdi. Both assured the Americans that they could handle any problem that arose. Bazargan likened the embassy takeover to a sit-in at an American university that would be over in a few days. Several days later, Bazargan resigned. An opponent of the hostage taking, he had held little power in the Khomeini government before the embassy seizure.

With Bazargan now out of the picture, the Carter administration was suddenly without a highly placed confidant in Tehran. The United States was adrift on the waves of Iran's revolutionary storm.[51]

The revolution ultimately destroyed what had long been the principal pillar of U.S. foreign policy in the region. The local power on which the United States had relied for maintaining secure access to the oil of the Persian Gulf was transformed overnight into a determined adversary.[52] The change had achieved the absolute worst-case scenario.

What factors contributed to the inability of the United States to act forcefully to preserve its vital interests? Robert Tucker points out that the circumstances in which the Carter administration came to power "did not dictate the foreign policy it followed during its first three years [1977–80] in office." Since external conditions did not dictate a particular foreign policy, it can be argued that the administration "acted as much from internal conviction—not domestic political necessity—as the Johnson Administration did in its pursuit of the war in Vietnam," thus contributing to a serious decline in the nation's global stature.[53]

In defending Carter's foreign policy, Cyrus Vance stated, "Much of the current dissatisfaction with the world and our role in it rests on certain fallacies. . . . " One such fallacy, he said, is that "America could have the power to order the world just the way we want it to be." The realization that the United States in fact lacked this power gave rise to the fear that "we are no longer capable of shaping our future."[54] But it seems irrefutable that the Carter administration could have done a better job of influencing events in Iran. Its failure to do so, said Tucker, is associated with "the visible decline of American power and position that has led today to a greater dissatisfaction over foreign policy then we have experienced for a decade."[55]

With the embassy takeover, noted Pierre Salinger, the most powerful government in the world found itself at the mercy of a country in revolutionary disorder. Some observers might cite the decision to admit the shah to the United States as the prime cause of the dilemma, but in fact the main problem was opportunities that were missed as a result of Carter's own ambivalence.[56]

Of Carter's response to the embassy takeover and hostage seizure, Milani writes: "President Carter's policy during the early phase of the crisis was inconsistent and indecisive. He granted sanctuary to the shah, an old ally—a move that was surely justifiable on moral and humanitarian grounds. But his decision to force the dying shah out of the United States [to Panama] was morally indefensible and politically imprudent. It exposed his inability to withstand pressure and made the Students Following the Imam's Line more belligerent. These two factors prolonged the crisis and contributed to Carter's defeat in the presidential election of 1980."[57]

The Carter administration was hapless, conflicted, insensitive to political currents in Iran, and inconsistent in its decision making. While sympathy must be expressed for Carter's dilemma regarding the admission of the shah to the United States for medical treatment, the president's expulsion of the Iranian monarch to Panama is deplorable on both moral and political grounds. Shooing the shah ignominiously off to Panama emboldened the militant students in Iran, who viewed the action as illustrative of Carter's weakness under pressure.

If an administration must take responsibility for what happens in the course of its tenure, "it is not surprising, then, that the Carter Administration has had to bear a heavy onus for the developments that have occurred since it came to office," wrote Tucker.[58] In the adverse outcomes of these developments, he added, could be found "even a kind of poetic justice at work," since rarely in recent American history has an administration "been as anxious to disavow the efforts of its predecessor and to proclaim 'new beginnings' as this one."[59]

The Carter administration cannot be absolved of its errors because it acted with good intentions. In the realm of foreign policy, this White House was characterized more by what has been called "an immoderate optimism" than by noble intentions. With respect to Iran, notes one observer, the administration gave the impression that it had "considered the consequences of its initiatives" and was persuaded that "the price to be paid for its policies was very modest."[60] As it turned out, the price was high.

This same immoderate optimism applied to the centerpiece of the administration's foreign policy, human rights. The Carter team was convinced that a human rights–based foreign policy would be beneficial both at home and abroad and would have few if any liabilities. Events would demonstrate, however, that far from being a win/win proposition, such a policy could conflict directly with "the integrity of strategic interests to which the Administration was presumably committed," in the words of Robert Tucker.[61]

By the end of 1979 it was evident that the Carter administration's foreign policy, especially toward Iran, had largely failed. Secretary of Defense Brown intimated as much when he said, "We must decide now whether we intend to remain the strongest nation in the world . . . " or to become a nation with "more of a past than a future."[62] The United States' stature had undeniably slipped.

The effects of the Iranian revolution reverberated not only within the United States, but across the volatile Middle East region, which duly noted that a broad-based revolt could succeed even against a government with strong ties to a superpower with which it had long been allied.

How badly had the United States misunderstood Iran? Says former Middle East correspondent Eric Rouleau, "From the very beginning of the Iranian Revolution, the West—and particularly the United States—seems to have been struck by a peculiar sort of political blindness."[63] Initially, the Carter administration failed to discern the early signs of revolutionary discontent, attributing increasingly explosive protests in the spring of 1978—first in Tabriz and then in Qum—simply to "obscurantist mullahs" who were hostile to the shah's agrarian reforms. The administration viewed ensuing demonstrations involving millions of Iranians, as well as strikes that affected factories, schools, universities, and oil fields and paralyzed the economy, as evidence mainly of fanaticism" rather than an irreversible uprising against the shah. What more could this spasm of turmoil signify, the U.S. government seemed to wonder, since it was merely the work of "a reactionary old

cleric" in revolt against a ruler who had sought to modern-
ize his country.

On March 11, 1980, a United Nations commission
left Iran without having made a deal for the hostages' release. In April, U.S. transport planes and helicopters landed
in the Iranian desert west of Tabas on a secret mission to
rescue the hostages. The outcome was disastrous. Two helicopters failed to function, and when the commander decided to abort the mission, a helicopter and a C-130 aircraft crashed. Eight American soldiers burned to death in
the flames. To Iranians the failure, broadcast widely on television, offered proof that a providential god had sanc-
tioned their revolution and interceded on their side.

Beset by the hostage crisis, Iraq's September 1980 invasion of Iran, and his rivalry with the fundamentalists,
Bani-Sadr struggled with the frustrating powerlessness of
his position. "In short, during the hostage crisis, the fundamentalists increased their anti-U.S. rhetoric," Milani reported. "They pushed the revolution toward radicalism,
and solidified their control over the revolutionary institutions, the state bureaucracy, and the armed forces, all to the
detriment of Bani-Sadr, who was turned into a figurehead
president."[64]

The secular rule of Bani-Sadr, who had swept to victory as president with more than 70 percent of the vote in
January 1979, was doomed. Immediately after his election
he had announced his intention to dissolve the Islamic
komitehs and militias as soon as he had reorganized the
armed forces, gendarmes, and police. The president, who
staunchly opposed the use of political violence for political ends, declared, "Denunciations, slander, torture, violence, massacres, prisons, are nothing more than manifes-

tations of a Stalinist society."[65] Khomeini, however, had cleverly endorsed the election of a secular president while handing the real reins of power over to the highly organized and resourceful Islamic clergy.

Bani-Sadr had little room in which to maneuver. His influence was severely limited by Khomeini's overwhelming authority. His protestations were cited as proof of his "Westoxication." Eventually, his enemies in the Revolutionary Council convinced Khomeini that if Bani-Sadr stayed in power, the very survival of the Islamic Republic would be threatened. A bitter Bani-Sadr felt betrayed. "I was like a child watching my father slowly turning into an alcoholic," he told a reporter. "The drug this time was power."[66] Finally, in June 1981, Khomeini dismissed Bani-Sadr, who had served for only 16 months as president. Bani-Sadr fled to France.

The Algiers Agreement resolving the hostage crisis was approved by the *Majlis* two days before President Ronald Reagan's inauguration, and the embassy hostages were released hours after Carter left office, on January 21, 1981. With Bani-Sadr as their spokesman, Iran's nationalists and leftists criticized the agreement, which had been negotiated solely by the fundamentalists. Under the terms of the accord, the critics pointed out, the United States made no apology for its past actions in Iran, the shah's wealth was not extradited, Iran's frozen assets in the United States were not recovered, and the hostages escaped the court trials that the Students Following the Imam's Line had demanded.

By June 1981 Khomeini was condemning all who opposed him. He vilified the National Front as "apostates," or enemies of God. He denounced Bazargan's Iran Freedom Movement and demanded that it dissociate itself from the National Front.

For Khomeini, one of the conditions of a successful revolution was its successful export. To this end his regime focused on the Persian Gulf states and Lebanon. The principal tools for exporting its revolution were the regime's army and Revolutionary Guard, propaganda, money, and subversion. This goal was formalized in the preamble to the constitution, which referred to the "ideological mission" of the army and the Revolutionary Guard to "extend the sovereignty of God's law throughout the world." According to the constitution, the basis for the mission could be found in a Koranic verse: "Prepare against them whatever force you are able to muster, and horses ready for battle, striking fear into the enemy of God and your enemy, and others beyond them."[67]

"The promotion and spread of revolutionary Islam was a primary foreign policy objective since the inception of Iran's new regime," says historian John Esposito. Esposito cites three bases for this objective: the Koran's directive that Muslims disseminate God's message throughout the world; the Islamic history of expansion and conquest, as illustrated by the extension of the Pax Islamica under Muhammad and his successors; and Iran's revolutionary constitution under Khomeini, which "explicitly proclaimed the Islamic rationale for an activist, aggressive foreign policy whose goal was the unity of the Islamic world and the extension of God's sovereignty throughout the world." He continues, "Ayatollah Khomeini espoused a nonsectarian or universalist Islamic revolution aimed at bridging the gap between Sunni and Shia Islam and liberating not just Shii Muslims but all the oppressed. A goal proclaimed by the new constitution was 'to perpetuate the revolution both at home and abroad.' "[68]

Another impetus was the hostage crisis, which precipitated a departure of Iran's foreign policy from the long-standing "equilibrium principle." This presumed that Iran would work within the international system, which included the two superpowers—the United States and the Soviet Union—and would pursue its self-interest by maintaining a balance of power in relation to other states. Under the new foreign policy, however, Iran rejected the superpowers' domination of the international system and resolved to export its revolution around the world.

The hostage crisis played a pivotal role in Khomeini's exhortation to export the revolution. Noting that the ayatollah had deemed the November 4, 1979, takeover of the U.S. Embassy and the subsequent collapse of the Bazargan government the "second revolution," Olivier Roy writes, "This second revolution . . . marked the transformation of Iran's foreign policy principle of equilibrium to one of a struggle between good and evil."[69]

Under the equilibrium principle, the shah's government had accepted the international system as legitimate and attempted to protect and promote Iran's national interest by maintaining a balance of power and influence in relation to other states. After the second revolution, the new regime's foreign policy makers questioned the very legitimacy of the existing international system; they sought to protect and promote Iran's Islamic interests by rejecting the dominance of both superpowers and by exporting the revolution throughout the world. Like Esposito, Ramazani notes that these last two principles are expressed in the new Iranian constitution, which was ratified in early December 1979.

The Afghan *mujahidin* (freedom fighter) movement, explains historian Olivier Roy, was a part of the surge in Islamic fundamentalism that occurred in the early 1980s. Like all mujahidin movements, the Afghan version sought the establishment of an Islamic state founded on the sharia and Muslim traditions. Noting that the fundamentalism in question is generally based on Sunni rather than Shii identity, Roy states that the Iranian revolution had only a minimal impact on the Afghan mujahidin other than the Shii minority; even in the latter case, he adds, "the assessment of the Iranian Shii influence has to be balanced."[70]

Shiites accounted for only about 15 percent of Afghanistan's population. Most were Persian-speaking Hazaras, poor peasants living mainly in the central part of the country. Following the Iranian revolution, Shiite political parties were divided among independent parties, pro-Khomeini parties, and a single party comprising former Khomeini adherents. To the extent that it existed at all, Iranian influence among the majority Sunni Muslims was cultural—the mujahidin adopted revolutionary rhetoric, and Iranian language and customs became more common—but not political. "It does not seem that Iran actually tried to implement a radical Islamic revolution among Afghan Sunni. . . . The most reasonable interpretation is strategic: Iran wanted to keep a foothold in Afghanistan through the Shii but was not eager to confront the Soviets or see a premature victory of the Mujahidin, which could bring the United States back to the area," says Roy.[71] Iranian radicals, he explains, suspected the mujahidin of conservatism and pro-Western leanings.

Consequently, Iran avoided direct assistance of the mujahidin against the Soviets, discouraged the mujahidin from seeking help from the United States, and reserved its support exclusively for the Shia, which limited Iranian influence in Afghanistan. "Iranian influence was also limited by the recent spread in Afghanistan of an Arab conservative fundamentalism, which strongly opposed both the Iranian revolution and the Shii mazhab (school of thought and legislation)," Roy adds.[72] This Arab fundamentalist wave gained strength after the Soviet invasion of Afghanistan in 1979 and intensified further after 1985. Its exponents included the Saudi Wahabbi sect, with which Osama bin Laden is associated, and the Muslim Brothers, both of whose followers entered Afghanistan through Pakistan.

It might be concluded that the Iranian revolution had negligible, if any, effects on the majority Sunni Muslims of Afghanistan. Iran influenced and supported the Shii minority until 1986, even clandestinely supplying military equipment at times, but Iran's efforts never approached the magnitude of Pakistan's support of the Afghan Sunni. Following the cease-fire ending its long war with Iraq, Iran pronounced its attempt to export its revolution to Afghanistan a failure. Eventually, the Pakistani-bred fundamentalist Taliban would prevail over the mujahidin in Afghanistan and offer refuge to Osama bin Laden.

Chapter 4

Afghanistan:
A Parallel Militant Universe

The revolutionary reverberations from Iran had barely subsided when a new tremor shook adjoining Afghanistan in December 1979, as the Soviet Union launched an invasion of its unstable, strategically important neighbor. The People's Democratic Party of Afghanistan (PDPA) regime of President Nur Muhammad Taraki and his politically adept prime minister, Hafizullah Amin, had seized power in a coup only a year earlier, overthrowing the government of Muhammad Daoud. The Taraki-Amin partnership was short-lived: in September 1979 Amin had Taraki killed, clearing the way for his own accession to the presidency. Amin issued a call for revolution, and fighting soon flared throughout the country.

The Soviet Union had poured aid and troops into Afghanistan, first in support of the Daoud government and more recently to stabilize the volatile state. President Leonid Brezhnev had conspired in the plot to replace Taraki with Amin, but now believed that Moscow's sizable investment in Afghanistan was threatened. The Kremlin suspected that Amin might not only be pro-American, but affiliated with the CIA, despite the latter's determination that Amin's PDPA was just the opposite: communist and pro-Soviet. In late 1979 Brezhnev acted decisively on his suspicions, launching an invasion in which Soviet forces murdered Amin and captured Kabul on Christmas Day. The Soviets soon installed Babrak Karmal, a founder of the PDPA, as head of the new government, but Moscow's intervention hardly produced stability, as a nationwide revolt spread across the beleaguered Muslim country.

How would the United States, reeling from its humiliating "loss" of Iran to Khomeini's still-unfolding Islamic revolution, react to the Soviet invasion of Afghanistan? What action might President Jimmy Carter take in the face of Brezhnev's provocative putsch? Would a wounded but perhaps wiser Carter respond in a way that would serve this country's best interests in the long as well as the short term?

The occasion presented the White House with an opportunity for "new" thinking. The reflexive response, dictated by "old" thinking, would be to oppose the rival superpower. Direct military confrontation was unthinkable in this case, as in most, although in his January 23, 1980, State of the Union Address, Carter threatened the use of such force as an element of the so-called Carter Doctrine for the Persian Gulf. The more likely approach would be to support Moscow's adversary, which in Afghan-istan meant the Islamic mujahidin resistance. The mujahidin included not only indigenous Afghan forces, but increasingly, as the jihad dragged on, Islamic militants from Arab nations throughout the region. But what would be the consequences of eventual success in Afghanistan by Islamic fundamentalists, who had already prevailed in Iran? Sometime in the future, might the United States rue the day it threw its weight behind such a force, only to abandon it after the goal of the Soviets' retreat had been achieved? Was the worldview espoused by Islamic fundamentalists compatible with the venerable American principles of democracy, freedom, and human rights—the very principles that the Carter administration considered the bedrock of its foreign policy?

New thinking, pursued outside the conventional Cold War framework, might suggest a different course. Such thinking would foresee the grave threat posed by the spread of Islamic fundamentalism. Drawing on the painfully fresh lesson of Iran, it would avoid entanglement with militant Islam. Such thinking would conclude that in 1979, embattled Afghanistan amounted to a win-win situation for the United States. The Soviets were likely to prevail over the mujahidin, or at least fight them to an inconclusive standstill, but at great cost in time, lives, and treasure. The probable outcome—a weakened Soviet Union, struggling to maintain a weak Moscow-friendly regime in Kabul against an Islamic resistance that was itself weakened by the attrition of a long, debilitating war—would serve U.S. interests admirably on all counts: win/win.

Unfortunately, old thinking, with ultimately disastrous consequences for the United States, carried the day in Washington. The Carter administration, propelled by National Security Adviser Zbigniew Brzezinski's conventional, Cold War perspective, opted to fight a proxy battle in Afghanistan. For most of the next decade the United States supplied hundreds of millions of dollars in aid to the mujahidin, whose ranks included Osama bin Laden, the Saudiborn heir to a construction fortune and an increasingly militant Islamist. (To avoid direct American involvement in the conflict and insure "deniability" for the CIA in the wake of its past abuses, all U.S. aid was channeled through Pakistan's secret military services agency, Inter-Service Intelligence [ISI], which coordinated the Afghan resistance effort.) The long war between the occupying USSR and the mujahidin ended in a stalemate. After the Soviets finally withdrew their troops, in 1989, the United States disengaged from Afghanistan, severing its ties to the Islamist resistance. The country descended into ruinous chaos, marked by violent ethnic and regional conflict, drug smuggling, and economic destitution.

The country, essentially abandoned by the international community, thus fell apart. Into the void of this "failed state" stepped the most militant of Islamic fundamentalists, the Taliban, led by a one-eyed cleric, Mullah Muhammad Omar, who would become bin Laden's comrade in arms (as well as his father-in-law). The Taliban consolidated their power through the early 1990s, and in 1996 proclaimed the establishment of the Islamic Emirate of Afghanistan, headed by Omar. As the guest of Omar's repressive regime, bin Laden would train the forces of his terrorist Al Qaeda organization at Afghan camps. When his native Saudi Arabia, the home of Islam's most sacred sites, Mecca and Medina, allowed U.S. forces to operate from its soil during the Gulf War of 1991, bin Laden turned vehemently against the United States, his onetime ally. The rest is lamentable history. The fatefully shortsighted U.S. policy, the result of threadbare old thinking, would bear terrible fruit in New York City, Washington, D.C., and Shanksville, Pennsylvania, on a bright September morning in 2001, more than two decades after Soviet tanks had rolled into Afghanistan.

In his book *Unholy Wars,* John Cooley, an American journalist who lived in and covered the Middle East for decades, traces what he calls "a strange love affair that went disastrously wrong: the alliance, during the second half of the twentieth century, between the United States of America and some of the most conservative and fanatical followers of Islam."[1] Characterizing the ten-year Afghan war between the U.S.-backed mujahidin and the Russian occupiers as the "centerpiece" of conflict in the region over the last quarter-century, Cooley observes, "In 2002, there is an ironic reversal of history: the United States and Russia, formerly Cold War enemies, have become de facto allies. Their common foe is what both perceive as a terrorist threat of near-cosmic dimensions from the same radical Islamists, and their successors and those trained by them, who fought and ruined Afghanistan in the 1979–89 war."[2]

The irony went deeper. It was cold warrior Brzezinski—who had fought hardest within the Carter administration to preserve the shah's reign in Iran, even advocating a coup by the Iranian military toward that end—who played a formative role in the administration's response to the Soviet invasion of Afghanistan. Brzezinski deemed the invasion a strategic threat to the United States; as it happened, Brzezinski himself may have helped to provoke that threat. In a 1998 interview with a French news magazine, the former national security adviser disclosed that, through a directive signed by Carter at his urging, clandestine CIA aid to the mujahidin had actually been authorized in July 1979—six months before the Soviet invasion, not afterward, as the official version of events had maintained.[3] This timeline has reportedly been confirmed by former CIA director Robert Gates.

Moreover, Brzezinski anticipated the consequences of the U.S. action: On July 3, 1979, the date on which Carter issued the directive, "I wrote a note to the President in which I explained to him that in my opinion, this aid would result in military intervention by the Soviets," Brzezinski told the French publication.[4]

In the same 1998 interview, at a time when the Taliban had solidified their control over Afghanistan, the Polish-born Brzezinski evinced a cavalier attitude toward the policy he had advocated and persuaded Carter to adopt: "Which was more important in world history? The Taliban or the fall of the Soviet empire? A few over-excited Islamists or the liberation of Central Europe and the end of the Cold War?"[5] In the end, Moscow's long and costly intervention in Afghanistan would probably have contributed to the collapse of the Soviet Union regardless of whether the United States decided to assist the mujahidin; Afghanistan's fragmented, multiethnic society and forbidding terrain have long been daunting obstacles, amounting to a Vietnam of sorts, to would-be conquerors. But the ill-fated U.S. alliance with militant Islamists—including the Taliban, which Washington initially supported as a potentially stabilizing force following the Soviet withdrawal—would turn out to have the worst possible consequences.

In fact, "another Vietnam" was precisely what Brzezinski and other architects of the U.S. policy—including, notably, Democratic Congressman Charles Wilson of Texas, a fervent advocate of aid to the mujahidin—hoped Afghanistan would become for the Soviet Union. Echoing a Vietnam-era theme, Brzezinski advanced a "domino theory" outlining the consequences should Moscow succeed. In his book *Power and Principle*, the national security adviser writes, "...in May 1979 I warned the President that the Soviets would be in a position, if they came to dominate Afghanistan, to promote a separate Baluchistan, which would give them access to the Indian Ocean while dismembering Pakistan and Iran."[6]

In retrospect, at least, Brzezinski's scenario appears seriously flawed, if not preposterous. Even if the Soviets had somehow managed to "dominate" Afghanistan, their ability subsequently to "dismember" (whatever that might mean) two other spacious, populous Muslim countries seems inconceivable. This was old thinking indeed. Worse, it was paranoid and delusional, ignoring the history of regional ethnic rivalries.

Meanwhile, Brzezinski's willingness to cultivate Islamic alliances in opposition to the Soviets seems feckless and unrealistic. In his book he recalls his promotion of a February 1980 proposal to form an Islamic government in Afghanistan should the Soviets withdraw from their troops. He writes, ". . . with the President's approval, I used various channels to suggest to some Islamic countries, and then later directly to our Western European allies, that the proposal be made to the Soviets that neutral Islamic countries create an international contingent which could replace the Soviet forces in Afghanistan, perhaps under UN auspices, and permit the restoration of a genuinely neutral but not violently anti-Communist government." Noting his belief that such an arrangement might encourage the Soviets to withdraw, he continues: "In the meantime, such an initiative would be likely to win endorsement even from the relatively anti-Western Islamic governments and thus help to shape a united Moslem front. As I noted in my journal on February 25, 'I do not exclude the possibility that the Soviets may eventually want to get out of Afghanistan, but only if for a longish period of time the West remains united, the Islamic world remains outraged, and the Afghani resistance persists. I will give a memo to that effect to the President."[7]

Brzezinski's musings are problematic because his 1998 revelations to a French journalist do not square with his account of the same events in his 1983 book. What is indisputable is that the Carter-Brzezinski policy, based on Cold War precepts, aligned the United States with Islamic fundamentalist groups in an effort to ensnare the Soviet Union in "another Vietnam"—an outcome that was likely without an American involvement that would ultimately have catastrophic ramifications.

* * *

What was the nature of the mujahidin resistance that the United States elected to support in Afghanistan? Shiites account for most of the Muslim population of Iran, but in Afganistan 80 percent of Muslims are Sunni and the remaining 20 percent Shiite. The role of the clergy, or ulama, differs markedly in the respective sects. Shiite Islamic clerics have an organized, hierarchical position in society and frequently engage in political affairs. In post-colonial Iran, Shiite ulama were moreover distinguished by their anti-Western views. In contrast, the societal role of Sunni clerics is relatively unstructured and, compared to Iranian Shiite counterparts, subordinate.

Sunni ulama have a relatively secular attitude toward politics, i.e., they acknowledge the legitimacy of a state as a separate entity and generally do not seek political power. Sunni Islamists in Afghanistan also harbored no animus against the West, believing that Western ideologies were the basis for the West's superior development and were a tool to be utilized in the formation of an Islam-based modern political ideology. These anticommunist Islamists viewed the Palestine Liberation Organization (PLO) with mistrust, regarding it as pro-Soviet.

As noted by analyst Olivier Roy in his book *Islam and Resistance in Afghanistan*, the Shiite minority in Afghanistan was heavily influenced by its brethren in neighboring Iran and played a discernible role in the resistance to the Soviet occupation. Shiite revivalist movements had arisen in Afghanistan in the 1950s and '60s, only to be suppressed by Daoud before his ouster in 1978. The later revival introduced Shiite youth groups to radical ideologies, including Maoism, and remnants of these groups participated in the insurgency against the Soviets. At the time of the Soviet invasion, observes Roy in the present tense, "...the influence of the Iranian revolution has been very marked amongst the young Afghan Shi'a since 1978, and this applies both to those who have worked in Iran and to those who are members of the clergy. They have adopted Iranian religious practices . . . and the politico-religious slogans of the revolution. Relations between the traditional clergy and young people who have returned from Iran are very tense."8

According to Roy, the mujahidin could be divided into three categories: permanently enrolled fighters, whose number was approximately equal to the 150,000 Soviet troops present in the country in 1983; part-time soldiers, who were called to action (usually by the political party to which they belonged) only in an emergency and otherwise tilled the land; and, potentially at least, every Afghan with a weapon who lived in a "liberated" part of the country. For the mujahidin, the ten-year struggle against the Soviets was a holy war, informed by the spirit of jihad.

* * *

Following the Soviets' 1980 appointment of Karmal as Afghanistan's new leader, aid to the mujahidin from Western and Islamic nations, including the United States and Saudi Arabia, began to flow through Pakistan's ISI. "The resistance movement began to receive substantial international assistance," writes Barnett R. Rubin in *The Fragmentation of Afghanistan*. "The Carter administration allocated $30 million for the program in 1980 and about $50 million in 1981. . . . In the fall of 1984 Congress took the initiative of nearly tripling the [Reagan] administration's 1985 request, to $250 million. Saudi Arabia approximately matched U.S. aid. Tens of thousands of fighters received military training in Pakistan. Some Shi'a mujahidin also received aid and training from Iran."[9] When Carter was voted out of office in 1980, he blamed Ronald Reagan for the continuing policy.

Soon after the Soviet invasion, Osama bin Laden was dispatched to Pakistan by Prince Turki ben Faisal al-Saud, the chief of Saudi intelligence, to explore the feasibility of forming an army of Arab volunteers to resist the occupation. Turki and bin Laden had developed a friendship based on their common concern about the decline of Islam as a political force, writes Cooley. In Pakistan bin Laden became acquainted with Abdallah Azzam, a Palestinian who was credited with inspiring the founding of the terrorist organization Hamas.

Cooley writes: "Azzam, in liaison with the generals running Pakistan's ISI, who were in turn under the direct command of President Zia al-Haq, outlined to bin Laden the need for weapons, transport and income for the families of the [mujahidin] fighters. Bin Laden promised to be generous with financing."[10] Well-educated and well-connected, bin Laden kept his promise, mounting a successful fund-raising campaign in Saudi Arabia that was helped by a $3 billion contract secured by his family's construction firm for restoration projects in Mecca and Medina.

"Delighted with his impeccable credentials, the CIA gave Osama free rein in Afghanistan, as did Pakistan's intelligence generals," Cooley reports. "They looked with a benign eye on a buildup of Sunni Muslim sectarian power in South Asia to counter the influence of Iranian Shi'ism of the Khomeini variety."[11] Reportedly, bin Laden was more than a mere patron of the Afghan resistance; he was an armed combatant against the occupying Soviet forces. Through his involvement in the conflict he nurtured a relationship with two of the principal Afghan mujahidin commanders, Gulbuddin Hikmatyar, a Pashtun, whose overriding goal of an Islamic revolution attracted Pakistani and Arab support and funding from the illicit drug trade; and Ahmed Shah Massoud, the Tajik leader of the Northern Alliance, a recipient of U.S. aid, and an eventual foe of bin Laden and the Taliban, who were implicated in his September 2001 assassination.

The Afghan war waxed and waned over its decade-long course, with both sides periodically mounting major offensives but neither ever gaining a conclusive advantage. In November 1986 the Soviet leadership decided to remove its troops from the conflict—a decision formalized in

Geneva accords signed in April 1988 by Afghanistan, the USSR, Pakistan, and the United States. The withdrawal would not be completed until February 1989. Meanwhile, in May 1987 the Soviets, in an effort to insure the presence of a friendly Afghan government after their exit, replaced Karmal with Muhammad Najibullah as president. A month later the Iranian government solidified an alliance among the eight Afghan Shiite resistance groups it had been supporting; in 1990, in response to the Soviet withdrawal, Iran merged the groups into a single party, to which it channeled its aid. Iran also supported Najibullah and his followers over a party endorsed by Saudi Arabia,which, along with Pakistan's ISI, favored Hikmatyar.

The politics of Afghanistan in the late 1980s and early 1990s were nothing if not labyrinthine. Shifting alliances were further complicated by the Gulf War, in which Pakistan, Saudi Arabia, and less radical mujahidin commanders supported the U.S.-led coalition, while Hikmatyar and similarly militant mujahidin leaders aligned themselves against the coalition. At the end of 1991 both the United States and the Soviet Union suspended aid to their respective Afghan clients and supported the formation of a UN-sponsored interim government to replace the Najibullah regime. As part of the ensuing plan, Najibullah resigned the presidency in April 1992. The new government proved impotent, however, and Afghanistan, ravaged by ten years of incessant warfare and now deprived of international humanitarian aid, sank into a morass of factionalism, lawlessness, anarchy, and violence.

Smuggling and heroin production—often controlled by Pakistani or mujahidin elements—flourished in the countryside, from which the intrusive Soviet troops had been removed. The spirit of jihad that had animated the mujahidin insurgency largely dissolved, as militias led by ethnic warlords fought for local or regional political power rather than Islamic solidarity. Meanwhile, increasing numbers of foreign militants appeared on the strife-ridden scene. Analyst Rubin observes, "As the Islamist fighters with foreign funding—and opium revenues—became even more autonomous from the local society, various forms of imported radical fundamentalism also grew, especially among eastern mountain Pashtuns. For the first time, large numbers of Arab radical Islamist 'mujahidin' entered the eastern provinces, strengthening nationalist resentments and extremist tendencies."[12]

* * *

Enter the Taliban, led by Mullah Omar, a Pashtun from Afghanistan's Qandahar province. The Taliban movement represented a long-standing phenomenon in Afghan history: Sunni Muslim teachers and students from rural madrasas (schools for Islamic studies) in Afghanistan and adjoining areas of Pakistan who embraced a fundamentalist strain of Islam. Many such men had joined the mujahidin jihad against the Soviets, and now Omar and his followers, buttressed by military aid from Pakistan, capitalized on the country's power vacuum. Displacing feuding warlords, the Taliban seized control of Qandahar in late 1994, offering its battered residents a concentrated source of order and authority while promoting civic and social institutions based on fundamentalist Islamic values. Their power base gradually expanded throughout the country. By early 1996 the Taliban had formed a centralized state, which they designated the Islamic Emirate of Afghanistan; by September of that year Kabul had fallen under their control; and by the summer of 1998 Omar's movement ruled most of the country, with the exception of northern regions controlled by Massoud.

The Taliban's new state apparatus set about establishing the fixtures of government, appointing administrators to supervise the country's provinces and localities; creating a nationwide judiciary of sharia courts, a security service (the Ministry of Enforcement of Virtue and Suppression of Vice) that tightly regulated daily life; and imposing order through actions such as the collection of weapons and the curtailment of opium trafficking. In accordance with the precepts of the Deobandi Islamic movement to which their leadership belonged, the Taliban also sought to exclude Shiite Muslims from political affairs and to marginalize the role of women in society.

Their religious ultraconservatism notwithstanding, the Taliban proved attractive, at least at the outset of their rule, to Pakistan and the United States. A reasonably orderly centralized state suited Pakistan's desire to maintain its influence in Afghanistan and American economic and political interests in the region. Writes Rubin, "At that time interest by several international corporations in oil and gas pipelines through Afghanistan also increased incentives for a centralized force to impose order. The United States regarded the Taliban as a force that might make Afghanistan more secure and enable U.S. companies to export gas and oil from Central Asia while maintaining sanctions on Iran. Hence Pakistan, initially with U.S. acceptance, supported the Taliban's growing aspirations to reconstruct a centralized state."[13]

In May 1996 Osama bin Laden returned to Afghanistan—rejoining his comrade Omar—from Sudan, where he had worked to forge a worldwide coalition of Islamic radicals. His Al Qaeda organization soon occupied a prominent position in Omar's Afghan regime, providing a well-trained and dedicated military force that the Taliban valued highly. As the regime's brutal, repressive practices progressively alienated it from the international community, its relationship with Al Qaeda, for which it provided training camps, and its affiliation with other foreign militant Islamic groups grew stronger.

"Bin Laden began to reorient the training of his troops in the al-Qaida organization," writes Cooley. "He moved away from more or less conventional anti-aircraft and anti-tank tactics used against the Soviets to urban guerilla warfare, sabotage and terrorism—also skills imparted by the CIA . . . to the Pakistani and Afghan trainers of the moujahidin—aimed at destabilizing the societies and governments which were soon to become his targets, mainly but not exclusively in North Africa, Chechenya, the Philippines and the United States."[14]

Afghanistan's reputation as a haven for Arab terrorists grew steadily in the 1990s, as Al Qaeda or associated groups were implicated in the 1993 bombing of the World Trade Center in New York, a 1996 assassination attempt on President Hosni Mubarak of Egypt, and the August 1998 bombings of U.S. embassies in Africa. In 1999 and 2000 the U.N Security Council passed resolutions imposing sanctions on the Taliban for harboring bin Laden, Al Qaeda, and other terrorist organizations.

The effects of bin Laden's refocused training of Al Qaeda—and of the failed U.S. policy in Afghanistan—came to awful fruition on the infamous date of 9/11/01. Writes Asia analyst Chalmers Johnson in a 2004 introduction to his book *Blowback*, "The attacks of September 11 descend in a direct line from events in 1979, the year in which the CIA, with full presidential authority, began carrying out its largest-ever clandestine operation—the secret arming of Afghan freedom fighters (mujahideen) to wage a proxy war against the Soviet Union, which involved the recruitment and training of militants from all over the Islamic world."[15] Following the Soviet withdrawal, he adds, the United States turned its back on its Islamic surrogate fighters, and eventually those surrogates responded in kind.

Due to the well-meaning though fatal mistakes of an American president, a once-benign Islamic movement established a legitimizing base in Iran, thus enabling it to metastasize into a transnational force that has changed the entire world. In addition, the United States' early support of the Afghanistan rebels created a veritable summer camp for terrorists.

In sum, it reads like a Greek tragedy, with mistakes repeated again and again. In the 27 years since, the United States has not recovered from the revolutionary reverberations in Iran that attempted to hijack one of the world's great religions. We now face a war without end.

Notes

Introduction

1. William Sullivan, *Mission to Iran: The Last U.S. Ambassador* (New York: W. W. Norton & Company, 1981), p. 114.

2. Ibid., pp. 147–48.

3. David S. McLellan, *Cyrus Vance* (Totowa: Rowman & Allanheld, 1985), p. 7.

4. Wesley G. Pippert, *The Spiritual Journey of Jimmy Carter* (New York: Macmillan, 1978), pp. 29-30.

5. Jimmy Carter, *Keeping Faith: Memoirs of a President* (Fayetteville: University of Arkansas Press, 1982), p. 145.

6. McLellan, *Vance*, p. 22.

7. Carter, *Keeping Faith*, p. 147.

8. McLellan, *Vance*, p. 23.

9. Ibid., p. 22.

10. Zbigniew Brzezinski, *Power and Principle: Memoirs of the National Security Adviser 1977–1981* (New York: Farrar, Straus, Giroux, 1983), p. 394.

11. Pierre Salinger, *America Held Hostage: The Secret Negotiations* (New York: Doubleday & Company, Inc., 1981), p. 5.

12. *Foreign Affairs*, Winter 1978/79, Vol. 57, No. 2, James A. Bill, "Iran and the Crisis of '78," p. 338.

13. Ibid., p. 339.

14. McLellan, *Vance*, p. 126.

15. Ibid., p. 126.

16. Cyrus Vance, *Hard Choices: Critical Years in America's Foreign Policy* (New York: Simon and Shuster, 1983), p. 328.

17. Ibid., p. 329.

18. Carter, *Keeping Faith*, p. 399.

19. Ibid., pp. 399-400.

20. Ibid., p. 400.

21. Vance, *Hard Choices*, p. 329.

22. Ibid., p. 331.

23. Salinger, *Hostage*, p. 31.

24. *Foreign Affairs*, 1979, Vol. 58, No. 3, Robert W. Tucker, "America in Decline: The Foreign Policy of Matu-

rity," pp. 467–68.

25. Mohammad Reza Pahlavi, *Answer to History*, (New York: Stein and Day, 1980), p. 14.

26. Ibid., p. 12.

27. George Lenczowski, *American Presidents and the Middle East* (New Haven: Yale University Press, 1988), p. 185.

28. Ibid., p. 226.

29. Ibid., p. 193.

30. Pahlavi, *Answer*, p. 18.

31. Burton I. Kaufman, *The Presidency of James Earl Carter, Jr.* (Lawrence: The University of Kansas Press, 1993), p. 132.

32. Fawaz A. Gerges, *America and Political Islam: Clash of Cultures or Clash of Interests* (Cambridge: Cambridge University Press, 1999), pp. 67-68.

33. Ibid., p. 68.

34. *Newsweek*, April 1990.

35. John Esposito and John O. Voll, *Islam and Democracy* (New York: Oxford University Press, 1996), p. 323.

36. Interview with Shah in Panama, 1979.

37. John Pynchon Holmes, *Terrorism: Today's Biggest Threat to Freedom* (New York: Kensington Publishing, 2002), p. 245-46.

Chapter 1

1. Milton Viorst, *In the Shadow of the Prophet: The Struggle for the Soul of Islam* (New York: Doubleday, 1998), p. 53.

2. Ibid., p. 53.

3. Richard Mitchell, *The Society of the Muslim Brothers* (New York: Oxford University Press, 1969), p. 297.

4. Ahmad S. Moussalli, *Radical Islamic Fundamentalism: The Ideological and Political Discourse of Sayyid Qutb* (Beirut: American University of Beirut, 1992), p. 103.

5. Peter L. Bergen, *Holy War, Inc.* (New York: Simon & Schuster, 2002), p. 51.

6. Adam Parfrey, *Extreme Islam: Anti-American Propaganda of Muslim Fundamentalism* (Los Angeles: Feral House, 2001), pp. 61–2.

7. John L. Esposito, *Unholy War: Terror in the Name of Islam* (New York: Oxford University Press, 2002), p. 58.

Chapter 2

1. William Shawcross, *The Shah's Last Ride* (New York: Simon & Schuster, 1988), p. 66.

2. Ibid., p. 60.

3. Ibid., p. 86.

4. Ibid., p. 87.

5. Ibid., p. 88.

6. Ibid., p. 112.

7. Hamid Algar, trans. *Islam and Revolution: Writings and Declarations of Imam Khomeini*, (Berkeley: Mizan Press, 1981), p. 169.

8. *Anti-American Terrorism and the Middle East: A Documentary Reader*, edited by Barry Rubin and Judith Colp Rubin (Oxford: Oxford University Press, 2002), p. 29.

9. Algar, *Islam and Revolution*, p. 181.

10. Ibid., p. 202.

11. Michael Ledeen and William Lewis, *Debacle: The American Failure in Iran* (New York: Alfred A. Knopf, 1981), p. 31.

12. Mohsen M. Milani, *The Making of Iran's Islamic Rev-*

olution (Boulder: Westview, 1988), pp. 107–08.

13. Ibid., p. 109.

14. Ibid., p. 110.

15. Ibid., Pahlavi, *Answer to History*, p. 152.

16. Ibid., p. 152.

17. Salinger, *Hostage*, p. 4.

18. Ibid., pp. 4–5.

19. Ibid., p. 5.

20. Ibid., p. 5.

21. Shawcross, *Last Ride*, p. 130.

22. *Foreign Affairs*, Bill, p. 329.

23. Ibid., p. 61.

24. Milani, *Islamic Revolution*, p. 118.

25. *Foreign Affairs*, Bill, p. 333.

26. Michael M. J. Fischer, *Iran: From Religious Dispute to Revolution* (Madison: University of Wisconsin Press, 2003), p. 199.

27. Sullivan, *Mission*, p. 203.

28. Manouchehr Ganji, *Defying the Iranian Revolution: From a Minister to the Shah to a Leader of Resistance* (Westport: Praeger, 2002), p. 39.

29. Sullivan, p. 204.

30. Viorst, *Shadow of the Prophet*, p. 184.

31. Ledeen, *Debacle*, p. 144.

32. Milani, p. 108.

33. Ledeen, p. 117.

34. Pahlavi, p. 165.

35. Ledeen, p. 163.

36. Ibid., p. 163.

37. Ibid., p. 164.

38. Ibid., p. 164.

39 Ganji, p. 40.

40. Sullivan, p. 212.

41. Ibid, p. 212.

42. Ibid., p. 223.

43. Ibid., p. 225.

44. Ibid., p. 226.

45. Ibid., p. 233.

46. Kaufman, p. 125.

47. Milani, p. 122.

48. Pahlavi, p. 26.

49. Brzezinski, p. 367.

Chapter 3

1. Ledeen, *Debacle*, p. 171.

2. Ibid., p. 175.

3. Ganji, p. 40.

4. Elaine Sciolino, *Persian Mirrors: The Elusive Face of Iran* (New York: Simon and Schuster, 2000), p. 53.

5. Eric Rouleau, *Foreign Affairs*, "Khomeini's Iran," fall 1980, Volume 59, No 1, p. 6.

6. Ibid., p. 6.

7. *Foreign Affairs*, Bill, p. 300.

8. Rouleau, p. 2–3.

9. Ibid., p. 5.

10. Sciolino, p. 54.

11. Ibid., p. 39.

12. Ibid., p. 51.

13. Ibid., p. 52.

14. Elaine Sciolino, *Foreign Affairs*, "Iran's Durable Revolution," Vol. 61, No. 1, Spring 1983), p. 894.

15. Baqer Moin, *Khomeini: Life of the Ayatollah* (New York: St. Martin's Press, 1999), p. 265.

16. Sciolino, *Foreign Affairs*, p. 895.

17. Milani, *Islamic Revolution*, p. 133.

18. Ibid., p. 162.

19. Ibid., p. 166.

20. Robin Wright, *In the Name of God: The Khomeini Decade* (New York: Simon and Schuster, 1989), p. 75.

21. Shaul Bakhash, *The Reign of the Ayatollahs* (New

York: Basic Books, 1984), p. 162.

22. Ledeen, p. 196.

23. David Frost Interview in Panama with Moham-mad Reza Pahlavi, 1979

24. Sullivan, *Mission*, p. 240.

25. Salinger, *Hostage*, p. 33.

26. Ibid., p. 34.

27. Ibid., p. 34.

28. Ibid., p. 28.

29. Bakhash, p. 73.

30. Ibid., p. 78.

31. Ibid., p. 79.

32. Salinger, p. 15.

33. Ibid., p. 17–18.

34. Ibid., p. 18.

35. Ibid., p. 19.

36. Ibid., p. 24.

37. Ibid., p. 25.

38. Ibid., p. 26.

39. Pahlavi, *Answer*, pp. 20–21.

40. Ibid., p. 27.

41. Milani, p. 165.

42. Ibid., p. 164.

43. Ibid., p. 164.

44. Ibid., p. 166.

45. Ibid., p. 171.

46. Rouleau, p. 8.

47. Ibid., p. 11.

48. Ibid., pp. 12–13.

49. Milani, p. 108.

50. Ibid., p. 129.

51. Ibid., p. 129.

52. Salinger, p. 29.

53. Robert Tucker, *Foreign Affairs*, Vol. 58, No. 3, "America in Decline: The Foreign Policy of 'Maturity,' " p. 449.

54. Robert Tucker, *Foreign Affairs*, Vol. 59, No. 2, "The Purposes of American Power," p. 243.

55. Ibid., p. 243.

56. Salinger, p. 31.

57. Milani, p. 178.

58. Tucker, "America in Decline," p. 457.

59. Ibid., p. 457.

60. Ibid., p. 465.

61. Ibid., p. 466.

62. Ibid., p. 468.

63. Rouleau, p. 481.

64. Milani, p. 179.

65. Rouleau, p. 14.

66. *Foreign Affairs*, Sciolino, p. 896.

67. Hamid Algar, trans., *Constitution of the Islamic Re-*

public of Iran (Berkeley: Mizar Press, 1980), p. 22.

68. John L. Esposito, ed., *The Iranian Revolution: Its Global Impact* (Miami: Florida International University Press, 1990), pp. 30–31.

69. Olivier Roy, *Islam and Resistance in Afghanistan,* (Cambridge: Cambridge University Press, 1990), p. 44.

70. Ibid., p. 179.

71. Ibid., p. 193.

72. Ibid., p. 195.

Chapter 4

1. John Cooley, *Unholy Wars: Afghanistan, America and International Terrorism* (London: Pluto Press, 2002), p. xiii.

2. Ibid., p. xv.

3. Interview with Brzezinski by Vincent Javert in *Le Nouvel Observateur*, January 15–21, 1998, p. 76; cited in Cooley, *Unholy Wars*, p. 10.

4. Ibid., p. 10.

5. Ibid., p. 11.

6. Zbigniew Brzezinski, *Power and Principle: Memoirs of*

the National Security Adviser, 1977–1981 (New York: Farrar, Straus, Giroux, 1983), p. 427.

7. Ibid., pp. 434–35.

8. Olivier Roy, *Islam and Resistance in Afghanistan* (Cambridge, U.K.: Cambridge University Press, 1990), p. 52.

9. Barnett Rubin, *The Fragmentation of Afghanistan* (New Haven: Yale University Press, 2002), pp. 180–81.

10. Cooley, *Unholy*, p. 202.

11. Ibid., pp. 202–03.

12. Rubin, *Fragmentation*, p. 183.

13. Ibid., pp. xiii–iv.

14. Cooley, *Unholy Wars*, p. 205.

15. Chalmers Johnson, *Blowback: The Costs and Consequences of American Empire* (New York: Henry Holt and Company, LLC, 2002), p. xii.

Bibliography

Abod, Geneive. *No God but God: Egypt and Triumph of Islam.* New York: Oxford Unviersity Press, 2000.

Abrahamian, Ervand. *Khomeinism: Essays on the Islamic Republic.* Berkeley: University of California Press,1993.

Abu-Rabi, Ibrahim M. *Intellectual Origins of Islamic Resurgence in the Modern Arab World.* Albany: State University of New York Press, 1996.

Algar, Hamid, trans., *Islam and Revolution: Writings and Declaration of Imam Khomeini.* Berkeley: Mizan Press, 1981.

_____. *Roots of the Islamic Revolution in Iran.* Oneonta: Islamic Publications International, 2001.

_____., ed., *Constitution of the Islamic Republic of Iran.* Berkeley: Mizan Press, 1980.

Ali, Tariq. *The Clash of Fundamentalisms: Crusades, Jihads and Modernity.* London: Verso, 2002.

Amnesty International. *Iran: Violation of Human Rights.* London: Amnesty International, 1987.

Ansari, Ali M. *Modern Iran Since 1921: The Pahlavis and After.* London: Longman, 2003.

Arjomand, Said Amir. *The Turban for the Crown: The Islamic Revolution in Iran.* New York: Oxford University Press, 1988.

Bakhash, Shaul. *The Reign of the Ayatollahs: Iran and the Islamic Revolution.* New York: Basic Books, 1984.

Beinin, Joel and Joe Stork., eds. *Political Islam: Essays from Middle East Report.* Los Angeles: University of California Press, 1997.

Bergen, Peter L. *Holy War Inc.: Inside the Secret World of Osama bin Laden.* New York: Free Press, 2001.

Bill, James A. *The Eagle and the Lion.* New Haven: Yale University Press, 1988.

Bodansky, Yossef. *The Man who Declared War on America.* Rocklin: Prima, 1999.

Bourne, Peter G. *Jimmy Carter: A Comprehensive Biography from Plains to Post-presidency.* New York: Scribner, 1997.

Brzezinski, Zbigniew. *Power and Principle: Memoirs of the National Security Adviser 1977-1981.* New York: Farrar, Straus, and Giroux, 1983.

Brinkley, Douglas. *The Unfinished Presidency: Jimmy Carter's Journey Beyond the White House.* New York: Viking, 1998.

Callahan, David. *Unwinnable Wars: American Power and Ethnic Conflict.* New York: Farrar, Straus, and Giroux, 1997.

Coll, Steve. *Ghost Wars: The Secret History of the CIA, Afghanistan, and Bin Laden, from the Soviet Invasion to September 10, 2001.* New York: Penguin, 2004.

Dajait, Hichem. *Europe and Islam: Cultures and Modernity.* Los Angeles: University of California Press, 1985.

Ebtekar, Massoumeh. *Takeover in Iran: For Inside Story of the 1979 U.S. Embassy Capture.* Vancouver, British Columbia: TalonBooks, 2000.

Esposito, John L. and John O. Voll. *Islam and Democracy.* New York: Oxford University Press, 1996.

———., ed. *Voices of Resurgent Islam.* New York: Oxford University Press, 1983.

Fischer, Michael M.J. *Iran: From Religious Dispute to Revolution.* Madison: The University of Wisconsin Press, 2003.

Friedman, Thomas L. *From Beirut to Jerusalem.* New York: Doubleday, 1995.

Ganji, Manouchehr. *Defying the Iranian Revolution: From a Minister to the Shah to a Leader of Resistance.* Westport: Praeger, 2002.

Gerges, Fawaz A. *America and Political Islam: Clash of Cultures or Clash of Interests.* Cambridge: Cambridge University Press, 1999.

Gettleman, Marvin E. and Stuart Schaar, eds. *The Middle East: An Islamic Reader.* New York: Grove Press, 2003.

Goldschmidt, Arthur, Jr. *A Concise History of the Middle East.* Boulder: Westview Press, 1999.

Griffin, Michael. *Reaping the Whirlwind: Afghanistan, Al Qa'ida and the Holy War.* Sterling: Pluto Press, 2003.

Gunaratna, Rohan. *Inside Al Qaeda: Global Network of Terror.* New York: Berkley Books, 2002.

Hefley, James, and Marti Hefley. *The Church that Produced a President: The Remarkable Spiritual Roots of Jimmy Carter.* New York: Simon and Schuster, 1977.

Hiro, Dilip. *The Essential Middle East: A Comprehensive Guide.* New York: Carol and Graf, 2003.

Hitchens, Christopher. *A Long Short War: The Postponed Liberation of Iraq.* New York: Penguin, 2003.

Hoge, Jr., James F., ed. *How Did This Happen? Terrorism and the New War.* New York: Council on Foreign Relations, 2001.

Holmes, John Pynchon. *Terrorism: Today's Biggest Threat to Freedom.* New York: Kensington Publishing, 2001.

Hourani, Albert. *A History of the Arab Peoples.* New York: Warner, 1991.

Huband, Mark. *Warriors of the Prophet: The Struggle for Islam.* Boulder: West View Press, 1998.

Jansen, Johannes J.G. *The Dual Nature of Islamic Fundamentalism.* Ithaca: Cornell University Press, 1997.

Jordan, Hamilton. *Crisis: The Last Year of the Carter Presidency.* New York: G.P. Putnam's Sons, 1982.

Juergensmeyer, Mark. *The New Cold War?: Religious Nationalism Confronts the Secular State.* Los Angeles: University of California Press, 1993.

Kakar, M. Hassan. *Afghanistan: The Soviet Invasion and the Afghan Response.* Los Angeles: University of California Press, 1995.

Karsh, Efraim & Inari Karsh. *Empires of the Sand: The Struggle for Mastery in the Middle East 1789-1923.* Cambridge: Harvard University Press, 2001.

Kaufman, Burton I. *The Presidency of James Earl Carter, Jr.* Lawrence: University Press of Kansas, 1993.

Keddie, Nikki R. *Modern Iran: Roots and Results of Revolution.* New Haven: Yale University Press, 2003.

Kepel, Gilles. *Jihad: The Trail of Political Islam.* Cambridge: Harvard University Press, 2002.

Khomeini, Ayatollah Ruhollah. *Islamic Government.* Arlington: Manor Books, 1979.

Kinzer, Stephen. *All the Shah's Men: An American Coup and the Roots of Middle East Terror.* Hoboken: John Wiley & Sons, 2003.

Kissinger, Henry. *White House Years.* Boston: Little, Brown & Company, 1979.

_____. *Years of Upheaval.* Boston: Little, Brown and Company, 1983.

Kreisberg, Paul H., ed. *American Hostages in Iran: The Conduct of a Crisis.* New Haven: Yale University Press, 1985.

Ledeen, Michael, and William Lewis. *Debacle: The American Failure in Iran.* New York: Knopf, 1981.

_____. *The War Against the Terror Masters.* New York: St. Martin's Press, 2002.

Lewis, Bernard. *The Crisis of Islam: Holy War and Unholy Terror.* New York: Random House, 2003.

Lindholm, Charles. *The Islamic Middle East: Tradition and Change.* London: Blackwell, 2002.

Mackey, Sandra. *The Iranians: Persia, Islam and the Soul of a Nation.* New York: Penguin Putnam, 2002.

Mango, Andrew. *Ataturk: A Biography of the Founder of Modern Turkey.* Woodstock: The Overlook Press, 2000.

Mansfield, Peter. *A History of the Middle East.* New York: Penguin, 1992.

Margolis, Eric S. *War at the Top of the World: The Struggle for Afghanistan, Kashmir, and Tibet.* New York: Routledge, 2000.

Marty, Martin E and R. Scott Appleby. *Fundamentalisms Observed.* Chicago: University of Chicago Press, 1991.

McLellan, David S. *Cyrus Vance.* Totowa: Rowman and Allanheld, 1985.

Milani, Mohsen M. *The Making of Iran's Islamic Revolution: From Monarchy to Islamic Republic.* Boulder: Westview Press, 1998.

Miller, Judith. *God Has Ninety-Nine Names: Reporting from a Militant Middle East.* New York: Simon and Schuster, 1996.

Mishal, Shaul, and Avraham Sela. *The Palestinian Hamas: Vision, Violence, and Coexistence.* New York: Columbia University Press, 2000.

Mitchell, Richard P. *The Society of the Muslim Brothers.* New York: Oxford University Press, 1969.

Moin, Baqer. *Khomeini: Life of the Ayatollah.* New York: St. Martin's Press, 1999.

Morris, Benny. *Righteous Victims: A History of the Zionist-Arab Conflict, 1981-1999.* New York: Knopf, 1999.

Morris, Kenneth E. *Jimmy Carter: American Moralist.* Athens: University of Georgia Press, 1996.

Moussalli, Ahmad S. *Radical Islamic Fundamentalism: The Ideological and Political Discourse of Sayyid Qutb.* Beirut: American University of Beirut, 1992.

Mottahedeh, Roy. *The Mantle of the Prophet: Religion and Politics in Iran.* New York: Simon and Schuster, 1985.

Murphy, Jr., John F. *Sword of Islam: Muslim Extremism from the Arab Conquests to the Attack on America.* Amherst: Prometheus Books, 2002.

Naipaul, V.S. *Among the Believers: An Islamic Journey.* New York: Random House, 1981.

Nojumi, Neamatollah. *The Rise of the Taliban in Afghanistan.* New York: Palgrave, 2002.

Pahlavi, Princess Ashraf. *Time for Truth.* United States: In Print Publishing, 1995.

Pahlavi, Farah. *An Enduring Love: My Life with the Shah.* New York: Hyperion, 2004.

Pahlavi, Mohammad Reza Pahlavi. *Answer to History*. Briar-cliff Manor: Stein and Day, 1980.

Parfrey, Adam, ed., *Extreme Islam: Anti-American Propaganda of Muslim Fundamentalism*. Los Angeles: Feral House, 2001.

Pintak, Lawrence. *Seeds of Hate: How America's Flawed Middle East Policy Ignited the Jihad*. Sterling: Pluto Press, 2003.

Pipes, Daniel. *In the Path of God: Islam and Political Power*. New York: Basic Books, 1983.

_____. *The Hidden Hand: Middle East Fears of Conspiracy*. New York: St. Martin's Griffin, 1998.

Qutb, Sayyid. *In the Shade of the Quran*. New Delhi: Islamic Book Service, 1998.

_____. *Milestones*. Cedar Rapids: The Mother Mosque Foundation.

_____. *Social Justice in Islam*. Oneonta: Islamic Publications International, 2000.

Rashid, Ahmed. *Taliban: Militant Islam, Oil and Fundamentalism in Central Asia*. New Haven: Yale University Press, 2000.

_____. *Jihad: The Rise of Militant Islam in Central Asia*. New Haven: Yale University Press, 2002.

Reeve, Simon. *The New Jackals: Ramzi Yousef, Osama Bin Laden and the Future of Terrorism.* Boston: Northeastern University Press, 1999.

Rockefeller, David. *Memoirs.* New York: Random House, 2002.

Roy, Olivier. *Islam and Resistance in Afghanistan.* Cambridge: Cambridge University Press, 1990.

Rubin, Barry and Judith Colp Rubin., eds. *Anti-American Terrorism and the Middle East.* Oxford: Oxford University Press, 2002.

Salinger, Pierre. *America Held Hostage: The Secret Negotiations.* Garden City: Doubleday, 1981.

Sciolino, Elaine. *Persian Mirrors: The Elusive Face of Iran.* New York: Simon & Schuster, 2000.

Shadid, Anthony. *Legacy of the Prophet: Despots, Democrats, and the New Politics of Islam.* Boulder: Westview, 2002.

Shawcross, William. *The Shah's Last Ride.* New York: Simon & Schuster, 1988.

Shlami, Avi. *War and Peace in the Middle East: A Concise History.* New York: Penguin, 1995.

Sick, Gary. *All Fall Down: America's Tragic Encounter with Iran.* Lincoln: iUniverse, 2001.

Sivan, Emmanuel. *Radical Islam: Medieval Theology and Modern Politics*. New Haven: Yale University Press, 1985.

Stern, Jessica. *Terror in the Name of God: Why Religious Militants Kill*. New York: Harper Collins, 2003.

Strasser, Steven. *The 9/11 Investigations: Staff Reports of the 9/11 Commission*. New York: Public Affairs, 2004.

Sullivan, Denis J. and Sana Abed-Kotob. *Islam in Contemporary Egypt: Civil Society vs. the State*. Boulder: Lynne Rienner Publishers, 1999.

Sullivan, William H. *Mission to Iran*. New York: W.W. Norton & Company, 1981.

Tanner, Stephen. *Afghanistan: A Military History from Alexander the Great to the Fall of the Taliban*. New York: Da Capo Press, 2002.

Tibi, Bassam. *The Challenge of Fundamentalism: Political Islam and the New World Disorder*. Los Angeles: University of California Press, 1998.

Vance, Cyrus. *Hard Choices: Critical Years in American Foreign Policy*. New York: Simon and Schuster, 1983.

Viorst, Milton. *In the Shadow of the Prophet: The Struggle for the Soul of Islam*. New York: Anchor, 1998.

Watt, W. Montgomery. *The Formative Period of Islamic Thought*. Oxford: Oneworld, 1988.

Wendell, Charles., trans., *Five Tracts of Hasan Al-Banna (1906-1949).* Berkeley: University of California Press, 1978.

Weaver, Mary Anne. *A Portrait of Egypt: A Journey Through the World of Militant Islam.* New York: Farrar, Straus, and Giroux, 1999.

Willis, Michael. *The Islamist Challenge in Algeria: A Political History.* New York: New York University Press, 1997.

Wright, Robin. *The Last Great Revolution: Turmoil and Transformation in Iran.* New York: Random House, 2001.

_____. *Sacred Rage: The Wrath of Militant Islam.* New York: Simon & Schuster, 1985.

_____. *In the Name of God: The Khomeini Decade.* New York: Simon & Schuster, 1989.